100 Ways to Develop Self Confidence

Published by :
Lotus Press Publishers & Distributors

100 Ways to Develop Self Confidence

Chitra Garg
(M.A., B.Ed)

Lotus Press
4735/22, Prakash Deep Building,
Ansari Road, Darya Ganj,
New Delhi- 110002

Lotus Press Publishers & Distributors
Unit No. 220, 2nd Floor, 4735/22, Prakash Deep Building,
Ansari Road, Darya Ganj, New Delhi-110002
Ph.: 41325510, 23280047, 098118-38000
E-mail: lotuspress1984@gmail.com
Visit us: www.lotuspress.co.in

100 Ways to Develop Self Confidence

ISBN: 978-81-8382-331-9

Printed & Published by: **Lotus Press Publishers & Distributors**, New Delhi -110002

Preface

There is a significant correlation between your social skills and your success in any area of life. With good social skills, it's easier to make friends, build strong relationships and get ahead in your career.

If you lack social skills, it's important to learn how to build social skills. If somebody asks you what would you like to improve about yourself? Although you may not want to admit it publicly I think a lot of us feel like we could use an improvement in self confidence.

There are actually quite a few practical tips you can use to raise your self confidence. As usual, with these tip-lists, don't try it all at once. Just try a few suggestions and see which ones work best for you. Some of them you'll need to practise a bit before they start to pay off.

It's like playing the guitar or cricket, it might not work too well the first or second time you try it. Keep in mind that you have a choice. You can choose if you want to raise or lower your self confidence.

Many of these suggestions can only boost your confidence temporarily. But this can allow you to do something you may not have been able to do before. And as you do it you build a deeper confidence in yourself. And collect concrete proof that you can actually do and achieve a lot of things.

Self confidence is the difference between feeling unstoppable and feeling scared out of your wits. Your Your perception of yourself has an enormous impact on how others perceive you. Perception is reality — the more self confidence you have, the more likely it is you'll succeed.

You want to be confident and feel confident, but what if you're starting with little or no confidence? True self-confidence isn't an overnight acquisition. It takes dedication to realize you are a good human being that is worthy of respect and love.

Friends, in this book I have tried to give you tips about gaining more and more confidence in a very simple way so that you may boost your confidence and gain success in life.

- Author

Contents

1. Self Confidence : An Introduction

"Confidence is a resolute state of mind by which you believe nothing is impossible."

Confidence is one of the most important qualities in a person's life to achieve success. Without confidence it is impossible to gain success for anybody in the world.

Today we live in a fast developing and competitive world. Everyone recognizes the crucial role of self confidence in the achievement of success. Confidence is the true fact of life based on which any impossible task can be completed with success. We can say that confidence is the key of the lock of life's success when once opened, can help to complete difficult, incomplete and impossible tasks.

Our mind is the wonderful creation of God. It takes decisions and makes us realize its importance. Sometimes our mind thinks positively about an event while at other times it starts thinking negatively. If anybody is in a state of confusion and indecisiveness, thereby it paves the way to supreme success.

With the help of confidence, you can learn the secrets of the world and use them according to your need. Many times your mind aspires to achieve success based on incomplete knowledge.

"You gain strength, courage and confidence by every experience in which you really stop to look fear in the face. You are able to say to yourself, 'I have lived through this horror. I can take the next thing that comes along.' You must do the things you think you cannot do."

-Eleanor Roosevelt

Faith upon oneself is called confidence. Faith is the most potent power given to human beings. Everyone possesses faith. However, it gets released only in certain conditions, or under specific junctures. Every miracle that is happening on Earth is owing to the power of faith.

In any human being more self-confidence can arise due to various reasons such as power, fame, strength, financial power, wealth, physical fitness and rank. But these are sometimes superficial contributory factors that make a person confident. It is not necessary that if they are successful in one field, they would be successful in other fields of life also.

Confidence means you're being who you are, authentically, for no other reason. No one gave you permission you just decided to be who you are. You decided to chase your dreams - that's confidence.

Believing in yourself and what you are doing, that's confidence.

2. Meaning of Self Confidence

Self-confidence means having the belief or the feeling of assurance that you will succeed and you can succeed in what you aim to achieve. Confidence comes from having a deep trust in yourself, in your abilities and commitment to achieve goal and perform tasks. Thus, your confidence stems mainly from your belief or faith in yourself and your abilities. As it is said, **"What the mind can conceive and believe and the heart desire, you can achieve if you have self confidence. The most difficult part is having that trust and belief continuously without self-doubt, fear and anxiety.**

It is myth that anyone is always confident or remains confident forever. Under certain conditions even the most confident people may lose their nerve. When provoked beyond tolerance, a person who is otherwise timid and nervous may show extraordinary courage. We can say that self-confidence stems from many natural factors, such as your appearance, education, knowledge, social and family background, past experiences, geographic and cultural factors, physical and mental health and social skills.

Having self-confidence is important to use the numerous opportunities you either create or get in your life to achieve success, peace and happiness. Unfortunately, many people lack self-confidence either totally or in specific areas, which prevent them from being effective and successful in their lives and careers.

Distinguishing qualities of confident person:

Self-confidence speaks for itself in your thinking and actions. A self-confident person has the following distinguishing marks:-

- Believes in what he or she does
- Has positive self-image
- Is willing to take risks
- Takes responsibility for his actions and their consequences
- Acknowledges his failures and mistakes and learns from them
- Has the heart to appreciate the virtues and achievements of others
- Is open to suggestions and ideas even if he does not agree with them
- Does not indulge in blame game and finding excuses and scapegoats
- Remains committed to his goals and dreams
- Listens to advise given by others but keeps his own Judgment
- Accepts complements and criticism graciously
- Never undermines his own abilities
- Does not put other people down to feel good
- Does not avoid responsibility for his life and actions
- Does not make decisions or perform actions to seek other people's approval.

3. Building Your Self Confidence is Important in Life

Anyone cannot build self-confidence by focusing on his confidence part alone. Your self-confidence is part of a mindset or your whole attitude. Therefore, to build self-confidence, you must notice some basic issues which prevent you from being your normal and confident self and use your full potentials to your best advantage.

You have to uncover the blockages that prevent you from being your natural self. It means you have to look deeper within to find the root causes, rather than dealing with the problem superficially. To build self-confidence, you have to understand the factors which contribute to it and build them. It means you have to spend time knowing yourself and increase your self-awareness.

Lack of Confidence

Any person who is lacking in self-confidence suffers from nagging self-doubts about himself, which shows up as fear of failure and rejection and anxiety about the outcome of his actions. He usually remains silent in a social conversation, readily agrees with the opinions of others. He hesitates to speak his mind. He does things to gain the attention and approval of others and waits for others to take the lead and make the decisions. He rarely takes risks or steps out of his comfort zone or ventures out to experience new and unfamiliar situations. Since he is afraid to stand for himself, he is not effective at negotiations. He keeps low expectations about himself and usually underperforms.

Success Comes With Confidence

Self-confidence is the difference between feeling unstoppable and feeling scared out of your wits. Your perception of yourself has an enormous impact on how others perceive you. Perception is reality – the more self confidence you have, the more likely it is you'll succeed.

Although many of the factors affecting self-confidence are beyond your control, there are a number of things you can consciously do to build self confidence.

Building your self-confidence is not a day's at work. It needs years and years of patience, dedication and perseverance. But good progress can only be done if the thoughts are moulded accordingly. To mould your thoughts into a perfect way, it is necessary for you to let loose your imagination till the thoughts develop into a specific pattern towards success.

Many people do not finish what they begin. Along the way they lose heart and become distracted. They give up a cherished dream that might have changed their lives.

Often you come up with innovative ideas or set a difficult goal for yourself, but do not find the courage to give them shapes. Generally you entertain certain wishes, hopes and dreams, but underperform in reaching them, because you lack courage and conviction, believing that you do not have the resources or the ability. In such cases success is denied to you because in some mysterious ways you hold back and deny yourself opportunities to achieve success and make a mark for yourself.

In short, you lack confidence in yourself, in what you think, believe and aim to achieve. So have self confidence, if you want to be successful in life.

Self-confident people have qualities that everyone

admires. Self-confidence is extremely important in almost every aspect of your life, yet many people don't find it. Sadly, this can be a vicious circle: People who lack self-confidence can find it difficult to become successful. Generally, most people are reluctant to back a project that's being pitched by someone who was nervous, fumbling and overly apologetic.

On the other hand, you might be persuaded by someone who speaks clearly, who holds his or her head high, who answers questions assuredly and who readily admits when he or she does not know something.

Self-confident people inspire confidence in others. They might be their audience, their peers, their bosses, their customers and their friends. And gaining the confidence of others is one of the key ways in which a self-confident person finds success.

The most important thing about self-confidence is that it can be learned and built on. And, whether you're working on your own self-confidence or building the confidence of people around you, it's well-worth the effort!

4. How Confident do you seem to Others?

Your level of self-confidence can show in many ways: your behaviour, your body language, how you speak, what you say and so on. Look at the following comparisons of common behaviours and find, which thoughts or action do you recognize in yourself and people around you.

If you are Self-Confident	If you are Low Self-Confident Person
Doing what you believe to be right, even if others mock or criticize you for it.	Governing your behaviour based on what other people think.
Being wiling to take risks and go the extra mile to to achieve better things.	Staying in your comfort zone, fearing failure and so avoid taking risks.
Admitting your mistakes, and learning from them.	Working hard to cover up misktakes and hoping that you can fix the problem before anyone notices.
Waiting for others to congratulate you on your accomplishments.	Trying to show your own virtues as often as poosible to as many people as possible.
Accepting compliments graciously. "Thanks, I really worked hard on that prospectus. I'm pleased you recognize my efforts."	Dismissing compliments off-handedly "Oh that prospectus was nothing really, anyone could have done it.'

Self-confident people are generally more positive – they believe in themselves and their abilities and they also believe in living life to the full. Low self-confidence can be self-destructive and it often manifests itself as negativity.

Self-confidence is about balance. At one extreme, we have people with low self-confidence, at the other end; we have people who may be over-confident.

If you are under-confident, you'll avoid taking risks and stretching yourself; and you might not try at all. And if you're over-confident, you may take on too much risk, stretch yourself beyond your capabilities, and then crash badly. You may also find that you're so optimistic that you don't try hard enough to truly succeed.

Getting everything right is a matter of having the right amount of confidence, founded in reality and on your true ability. With the right amount of self-confidence, you will take informed risks, stretch yourself, but not beyond your abilities and try hard.

5. Preparing for your Journey to Self Confidence

The first step involves getting yourself ready for your journey to self-confidence. You need to take stock of where you are, think about where you want to go, get yourself in the right mindset for your journey, and commit yourself to starting it and staying with it.

In preparing for your journey, you should know about following things:

1. Look at what you have already achieved in life

Think about your life so far and list the ten best things you've achieved in an "Achievement List." Perhaps you came top in an important test or exam or played a key role in an important team or produced the best sales figures in a period or did something that made a key difference in someone else's life or delivered a project that meant a lot for your business. Put these into a smartly formatted document, which you can look at often. And from now spend a few minutes each week enjoying the success you've already had!

2. Think About What's Important to You, and Where you Want to Go

Think about the things that are really important to you, and what you want to achieve in your life. Setting and achieving goals is a key part of this and real self-confidence comes from this. Goal setting is the process you use to set your targets and measure your successful hitting of those targets.

Set goals that exploit your strengths, minimize your weaknesses, realize your opportunities and control the threats you face. And having set the major goals in your life, identify the first step in each. Make sure it's a very small step, perhaps taking no more than an hour to complete.

3. Think About Your Strengths

Take a look at whom and where you are. Looking at your Achievement List and reflecting on your recent life, think about what your friends would consider to be your strengths and weaknesses. From these, think about the opportunities and threats you face.

Make sure that you enjoy a few minutes reflecting on your strengths!

4. Start Managing Your Mind

At this stage, you need to start managing your mind. Learn to pick up and defeat the negative self-talks which can destroy your confidence.

This teaches you how to use and create strong mental images of what you'll feel and experience as you achieve your major goals. There is something about doing this that makes even major goals seem achievable.

5. Commit Yourself to Success!

The final part of preparing for the journey to self-confidence and success in life is to make a clear promise to yourself that you are absolutely committed to your journey and that you will do all in your power to achieve it.

If as you're doing it, you find doubts starting to surface write them down and challenge them calmly and rationally. If they dissolve under scrutiny, that's great. However, if they are based on genuine risks, make sure you set additional goals to manage these appropriately.

Now you should follow the ways to develop confidence given in this book.

6. Have higher Self-Esteem

Self-esteem is a person's own evaluation of himself psychologically, emotionally, physically, and spiritually. Self-esteem is mainly about the worth we give ourselves, how much we like ourselves and how well we feel about ourselves.

Self-esteem is influenced by other sources such as friends, family and any significant other figures in our lives. If a person is told that he is 'not good enough' over a certain period of time by a close friend, colleague or teacher, it is likely this person will believe to some extent the criticism as 'truth'. We are often indulged into thinking that rich and successful people have got the highest levels of self-esteem. This however is an illusion. Our lives can be divided into different categories: Career; wealth and status, these are three particular categories. Self-esteem may be lacking in family, relationship and health categories. We are all human, so it follows that our self esteem will fluctuate throughout the different changes and challenges we meet in our lives.

Self-esteem is very precious in life. It makes you more confident in life. Your confidence directly stems from your self esteem. The higher self-esteem, the greater will be confidence. Self-esteem means your perception of your self-image and you're feeling self-worth. That means that how you perceive yourself, how you estimate your own image.

Your self-esteem depends practically upon the same factors as you self-confidence. You should always try to have your self-esteem at higher side. But this quality should not overpower your behaviour. You should behave very humbly with your self-esteem high.

Therefore, if you want to build self-confidence, you should first address your self-esteem issues. With positive self-esteem, you will naturally feel more confident. With your confidence you can win the heart of other people. The first step towards gaining self-confidence is to maintain self-esteem.

7. Why Is Self-Esteem Important?

Self-esteem is important because it gives you the peace of mind you need to appreciate your own life and the lives of others. Self-esteem brings a person joy, confidence, well being, and wholeness. A person with a good level of self-esteem has the ability to live life joyfully regardless of setbacks. The most important is, improving self-esteem is easy when a person realizes that she/he can take responsibility over his/her own thoughts feelings and behaviours. Improving self-esteem is as easy as taking up a small hobby such as reading. Learning to do self-esteem enhancing exercises will lead you toward a better and happier life.

Try to improve your self- esteem

You can simply begin today to work through some of the ideas and exercises listed here. Some of them might be more appealing to you than others as you read through the information. Be aware of how what you are learning and how you can incorporate it into your own life. Be sure and try to relax. There is no need to be anxious about the difficulties. If you do feel a little anxious through, remember that this is only because you want what's best for yourself.

8. Try to gain knowledge and competence

Did you ever realize, knowledge, competence and self-confidence go together? If you try to realise, you will find it true. If you have more knowledge and competence about something you will become more confident in that particular area. *For example,* if you are good in mathematics, you will always be more confident when there is a discussion about any calculation or any figure.

For example, if you have low self confidence in your job, it may be because you are lacking the information and knowledge of how to perform well.

Competency in anything can always be developed via preparation, practice and experience. The key to developing competency is to engage in knowledge acquisition and repeatedly do it to the point you can. *For example,* if it's an academic subject, read up as much as you can through different sources, if it's a sport or technique, keep training every day, if it's giving a presentation or public speaking, continuously practice in front of different audiences to build up the skill sets. In the same way if it's something social like talking to a stranger, just start with small goals of talking to one stranger every day. Eventually, you will find yourself so competent in the area that you become naturally self-confident in it.

Some people seek knowledge and competency to gain status symbols and titles. Some people strive for successes in everything they do. The problem with acquiring symbols of worth to increase self-confidence is the boost in self-confidence. But it only lasts as long as the symbols are valid.

If they were to be removed from you or lose their relevance, your self-confidence will change accordingly.

Imagine a badminton player who measures his worth based on his victories in his badminton games. He keeps practicing to increase his odds of victories. Whenever he wins, his self-confidence gets a boost; however whenever he loses, his self-confidence gets a hit.

If you really want to gain knowledge, you have to get close attachment with learned people. You have to ask questions and learn from them. You must be enthusiastic to do this. Read as many books as you can. Connect to the internet for best webs that can give you good knowledge. Meet experienced people and talk to them that are the best way to gain knowledge.

9. Improve Your Willpower

What willpower is and how it works in the brain

Willpower is a response that comes from both the brain and the body.

The willpower response is a reaction to an internal conflict. You want to do one thing, such as smoke a cigarette or eat other person's lunch, but know you shouldn't. Sometimes you know you should do something, like file your taxes or go to the gym, but you'd rather do nothing.

One of brain's parts helps us with things like decision-making and regulating our behaviour. Self-control, or willpower, falls under this heading, and thus you should take care of the brain.

To be effective at controlling your making of sound decisions, section of brain, the prefrontal, cortex needs to be looked after. That means feeding it with good-quality food so it has enough energy to do its job and getting enough sleep.

While trying to control your temper, you should ignore distractions and refuse anger. You can look at willpower like a muscle, it can get exhausted by overuse, but just like our physical muscles, there are some researchers who believe we might be able to strengthen our willpower by training it.

How can you increase your willpower?

Even if you have much willpower stress and normal self-control depletes your resource. You can do the following things for increasing the pool of willpower.

1. **You should encourage yourself to stick to your plan.**

Self-affirmation can even help you to have more self-control when you're running out. A good example of this is the difference between telling yourself "I can't" and "I don't."

Everytime you tell yourself "I can't", you're creating a feedback loop that is a reminder of your limitations. This terminology indicates that you're forcing yourself to do something you don't want to do. So try telling yourself that you 'don't do' that bad habit, rather than punishing yourself by saying "I can't."

2. **You should Increase your capacity for pressure you should learn how to manage.**

According to specialists, stopping to take a few deep breaths when you feel overwhelmed or tempted can be a great start in managing your stress levels and improving your willpower.

3. **You should get more sleep to help your brain manage energy better.**

Sleep deprivation (even just getting less than six hours a night) is a kind of chronic stress that impairs the body and brain energy.

4. **You can meditate to increase willpower.**

Meditation has also been linked to increasing the reserve of willpower we have available, as well as improving attention, focus, stress management and self-awareness.

5. **You should focus on things what's important now** and postpone things for later to gain attention.

6. **You should do exercise and get good nutrition:** This is the most ignored route to higher willpower. This is great way which is often easily undervalued. The thing that can

make you a lot more resilient to stress, and thus boost willpower, is regular physical exercise. Both relaxing and mindful exercise like yoga and intense physical training can provide these benefits.

Not only will exercise and good nutrition improve your willpower, but they'll make you feel better as well. Exercise in particular is known for making you happy by releasing toxins. This tends to minimize the discomfort of exercise, block the feeling of pain and is even associated with a feeling of euphoria.

10. Try to Use Your Imagination to Create the Self You Want

Imagination plays a big role in creating your self-confidence. Try filling your mind with thoughts of not letting other people's negative voices affect your self-confidence. Develop an attitude of not letting their negative opinions or actions destroy your self-esteem.

When someone gives you a negative opinion, you can accomplish more by not getting discouraged. Knowing that an opinion is nothing more than a comment of what, or how, a person feels and believes, is also important.

You can use your mind as a blank sheet of paper that gives you the chance to create new goals, and to reach for new heights. A blank page can give you an important guide that pushes you toward self motivation and inspiration. You can change your blank page at any time.

God has given you imagination for you to use and to create the business and personal life you want. You can create a new beginning. It's your choice and not anyone else's. You can use it to erase any negative thoughts, feelings, or opinions. In this way when you success you gain self-confidence.

When someone tells you can't do something. Is it possible for you to separate the fact of their statement from their opinion? You should use your imagination to create a better, more useful outcome. Understanding that there is a great distinction between the two may decide your success or failure.

Being able to determine the difference between facts and

opinions when you hear them is important. Always try to consider the cost of having someone else's opinion prevent you from doing something that is not based on facts. Are the opinions more important than your desire to be the self you want?

This is like knowing that just because it's raining outside, it has to be a bad day. One is fact; the other is an opinion. Use this guidance whenever you find yourself hesitating to make a decision in your personal life or in your business life.

Another good defence mechanism would be to build up a series of little successes. Even small success will build the confidence and self-esteem that you need for bigger and better success in your business and your personal life.

Use your imagination to succeed and to create the self you want. After all, imagination is the power of the mind to form images – good, bad, or indifferent; positive, loving, or negative; funny, sad, or happy. Which ones do you choose?

Imagine yourself succeeding. With the little successes that you accomplish, remember to give yourself credit to feel good about them. Prepare your mind for the bigger success. Then, build on the confidence and the strength that comes from succeeding.

11. Recognise the Types of Fears

"The way to develop self-confidence is to do the thing you fear."

William Jennings Bryan

When you have time, take a personal inventory of the fears keeping you from living the life you want. Then make a commitment and challenge yourself to face and conquer one that has been holding your back. Use the tips to guide your way. To get started, see if any common fears from the list below fit you.

1. Doing something you've never done before
2. Admitting mistakes or wrong-doings
3. Acceptance of being inadequate/not good enough
4. Healing emotional wounds
5. Health concerns
6. Money/finances never having enough.
7. Expressing yourself as 'Failure'
8. Public speaking
9. Taking a risk, such as starting or changing careers
10. Saying "No" to others
11. Sharing your feelings

Short and easy ways to conquer your fears:

1. You should recognize a fear is present.
2. You should declare you are going conquer the fear.
3. You should focus your attention on goal.
4. You should motivate yourself with affirmations.
5. You should step into the fear with confidence.
6. You can consider copying a style you like until you find your own style.
7. Pat yourself on the back when it's over.
8. You will notice how much easier it gets.
9. The way to develop self-confidence is to do the thing you fear.

12. Learn To Face Your Fears

"The way to develop self-confidence is to do the thing you fear."

-William Jennings Bryan.

Self-confidence is belief in yourself. It is your ability to trust your abilities. The reason for lack of self confidence can almost always be summed up in one word-fear. This could be fear of embarrassment, fear of rejection, fear of criticism, fear of failure, or one of many other kinds. The key to building self-confidence is to face the underlying fear, and to practice doing that until you have successfully conquered your fear.

But to be frank, if you don't face your fears you won't experience any better self- confidence on a deeper and more fundamental level. Having experiences where you face your fear is what really builds self-confidence. There is no way around it. Here are few tips to conquer your fear:–

1. Take risks and set out to do what your heart desires. When you get the choice to sit it out or dance, choose to dance. The single most important thing you can do to build self-confidence, is to go ahead and do what you fear.

2. You should relax your fear away by relaxing your body. Psychological studies suggest that it is impossible to feel fear when the muscles of the body are kept perfectly relaxed. The moment you recognize fear or anxiety creeping in during a situation, identify those tightening muscles and try to focus on relaxing them.

3. You should practice reacting aggressively and positively towards fears in your imagination. Do this every time fear creeps into your imagination. It will be a matter of time before those reactions extend to reality when those or similar situations show up in your actual, day-to-day life.

4. You should substitute the feeling of fear with another "positive or feel good" feeling. You should think about anything that strikes the chord and leaves you with a pleasant taste. Capture that feeling, and replace fear with it.

As soon as you identify a negative thought creeping into your mind, change your internal dialogue to reverse the thought and put a positive spin to it. The moment you identify any irrational "what ifs" in your mind, replace them with "I'll handle it" or "It can be done" or "I'll figure it out". You will be more and more confident with this feeling.

5. You should act as if it were impossible to fail. When you set out to do what your heart desires, follow your inner voice, "Just Do it". Know that it can be done and you can do it: You just need to invoke that ability in you that will enable you to do so. If a mistake happens along the way, do not dwell; just correct your actions as you go along. You will feel confident. This will be your success.

6. Conquering your fear, one by one, builds confidence and increases your quality of life. Don't let your fears hold you back from living the life you wish you were living.

7. You gain strength, courage and confidence by every experience in which you really stop to look fear in the face. You are able to say to yourself. I have lived through this horror. I can take the next thing that comes along. You must do the thing you think you cannot do.

8. But to be frank, if you don't face your fears you won't experience any better self-confidence on a deeper and more fundamental level. Having experiences where you face your fear, really build self-confidence. There is no way around it.

9. However, there are ways to face your fears that do not include that much shaking of the knees. There are ways to make it easier for yourself.

10. You should realize that fear is often based on unhelpful interpretation. As humans we like to look for patterns. The problem is just that we often find negative and not so helpful patterns in our lives based on just one or two experiences or by misjudging situations, or through some silly miscommunication. When you get too identified with your thoughts you'll believe anything they tell you. A more helpful practise may be to not take your thoughts too seriously.

11. You should be curious. When you are stuck in fear you are closed up. You tend to create division in your world and mind. You create barriers between you and other things/ people. Curiosity is filled with anticipation and enthusiasm. It opens you up. When you are open and enthusiastic, you have more things to think about than focusing on your fear. One way is to remember how life has become more fun in the past. Try to remember all the cool things it helped you to discover and experience.

To be frank, if you don't face your fears you won't experience any better self confidence on a deeper and more fundamental level. Having experiences where you face your fear is what really builds self confidence. There is no way around it.

13. Develop Good Problem Solving Skills

Everybody can benefit from having good problem solving skills as all persons encounter problems on a daily basis. Some of these problems are obviously more severe or complex than others.

It would be wonderful to have the ability to solve all problems efficiently and in a timely fashion without difficulty. Unfortunately there is no single way in which all problems can be solved.

Although planning and structuring can help and make the problem solving process more likely to be successful. Good judgment and an element of good luck ultimately determines, whether problem solving was a success or not.

You should remember that relationships and businesses fail because of poor problem solving skills.

This is often due to either problems not being recognised or being recognised but not being dealt with appropriately. Solving a problem involves a certain amount of risk-this risk needs to be weighed up against not solving the problem.

The measure of success is not whether you have a tough problem to deal with, but whether it is the same problem you had last year.

14. Improve Communication

Developing Effective Communication Skills can lead to develop more self -onfidence. Effective communication is a key interpersonal skill and by learning how we can improve our communication has many benefits.

Communication is a two way process so improving communication involves both how we send and receive messages.

Effective communication skills are fundamental to success in many aspects of life. Many jobs require strong communication skills. People with improvedcommunication skills usually enjoy better interpersonal relationships with friends and family.

Following skills can help you further improve your communication skills:

1. You should be aware of other people's emotions. You should be sympathetic to other people's misfortunes and congratulate their positive landmarks. To do this you need to be aware of what is going on in other people's lives. Make and maintain eye contact and use first names where appropriate. Do not be afraid to ask others for their opinions as this will help to make them feel valued.

2. Consider the emotional effect of what you are saying and communicate within the norms of behaviour acceptable to the other person.

3. You should learn to listen. Listening is not the same as hearing. Learn to listen means not only to the words being spoken but how they are being spoken and the non-verbal messages sent with them. Try not to think about what to say next whilst listening. Your friends, colleagues and other acquaintances will appreciate good listening skills.

4. You should praise and encourage others. You can offer words and actions of encouragement, as well as praise, to others. Make other people feel welcome, wanted, valued and appreciated in your communications. If you let others know that they are valued, they are much more likely to give you their best. Try to ensure that everyone involved in an interaction or communication is included through effective body language and the use of open questions.

5. Learn how to Empathise. Empathy is trying to see things from the point-of-view of others. When communicating with others try not to be judgemental or biased by preconceived ideas or beliefs, instead view situations and responses from the other person's perspective. Stay in tune with your own emotions to help enable you to understand the emotions of others.

If appropriate, offer your personal viewpoint clearly and honestly to avoid confusion. Bear in mind that some subjects might be taboo or too emotionally stressful for others to discuss.

15. Learn To Speak Effectively

Do not say the first thing that comes into your head but instead take a moment and pay close attention to what you say and how you say it. Focus on the meaning of what you want to communicate or tell other persons.

You should aim to increase understanding by considering how your message might be received by the other person. By communicating clearly, you can help avoid misunderstandings and potential conflict with others. By speaking eloquently you will come across as more intelligent and mature.

Be aware of the messages you are sending via non-verbal channels: Make eye contact and avoid defensive body language. Pay particular attention to differences in culture, past experiences, attitudes and abilities before conveying your message. Explain things as simply as possible. Request clarification if unclear about a message. Always avoid racist and sexist terms or any language that may cause offence. If you speak effectively and convey your feeling successfully, you feel very confident.

16. Improve Your Behaviour

To be loved by all is everyone's wish. It boosts confidence. For your attitude try to do following things:

1. You should treat people equally. Always aim to communicate on an equal basis and avoid patronising people. Do not talk about others behind their backs and try not to develop favourites.

If you treat people as your equal and also equal to each other you will build trust and respect. Check that people understand what you have said to avoid confusion and negative feelings. If confidentiality is an issue, make sure its boundaries are known and ensure its maintenance.

2. You can use humour to be charismatic. Laughing releases endorphins that can help relieve stress and anxiety. Most people like to laugh and will feel drawn to somebody who can make them laugh. Don't be afraid to be funny or clever, but do ensure your humour is appropriate to the situation. Use your sense of humour to break the ice, to lower barriers and gain the affection of others. By using appropriate humour you will be perceived as more charismatic.

3. You should maintain a positive attitude and smile. Few people want to be around someone who is frequently miserable. Do your best to be friendly, upbeat and positive with other people. Maintain a positive and cheerful attitude to life. When things do not go to plan, stay optimistic and learn from your mistakes. If you smile often and stay cheerful, people are more likely to respond positively to you and would want to be around you. This will develop a feeling of confidence in you.

4. You should attempt to Resolve Conflict – Many times conflicts arise between friends and relatives. Learn to troubleshoot and resolve problems and conflicts as they arise. Learn how to be an effective mediator and negotiator. Use your listening skills to hear and understand both sides of any argument - encourage and facilitate people to talk to each other. Try not to be biased or judgmental but instead ease the way for conflict resolution.

17. You should Minimise Stress

Some scenarios are, by their nature, stressful. Stress can however be a major barrier to effective communication. All persons should try to remain calm and focused. To minimise you stress you should complain only when absolutely Necessary.

People will not be drawn to you if you are constantly complaining or whinging. If something makes you angry or upset, wait for a few hours and calm down before taking action. If you do complain, do so calmly, try to find some positive aspects to the situation and avoid giving unnecessary criticism.

18. Learn Dealing with Criticism

Dealing with criticism positively is an important life skill. At some point in your life you can be criticised, perhaps in a professional way. Sometimes it becomes difficult to accept, but that all depends on your reaction.

You can either use criticism in a positive way to improve, or in a negative way that can lower your self-esteem and cause stress, anger or even aggression.

To deal with criticism positively you require good self-esteem and some assertiveness skills.

It is wisely said-

"Any fool can criticize, condemn, and complain but it takes character and self control to be understanding and forgiving."

When challenged by another person, it is common to react in a negative manner. The way in which you choose to handle criticism has a knock-on effect in various aspects of your life. Therefore, it is better to identify ways in which you can benefit from criticism and use it to your advantage to be a stronger and more able person.

There are two types of criticism - constructive and destructive – learning to recognise the difference between the two can help you deal with any criticism you may receive.

What is constructive and destructive criticism?

The difference between constructive criticism and destructive criticism is the way in which comments are delivered. Although both forms are challenging your ideas, character or ability, you should take your criticism easily.

When someone is giving destructive criticism it can hurt your pride and have negative effects on your self-esteem and confidence. Destructive criticism is often just thoughtlessness by another person, but it can also be deliberately malicious and hurtful. Destructive criticism can, lead to anger and or aggression.

Constructive criticism, on the other hand, is designed to point out your mistakes, but also show you where and how improvements can be made. Constructive criticism should be viewed as useful feedback that can help you improve yourself rather than put you down. When criticism is constructive it is usually easier to accept, even if it still hurts a little.

In either scenario always try to remember that you can use criticism to your advantage. A proverb says –

A man who refuses to admit his mistakes can never be successful.

19. Don't be Critical Every Time

Some individuals are critical by nature and do not always realise that they are hurting the feelings of another person. It is a fact that nobody likes such persons. So you should not be critical every time.

If you know a person who is critical of every time, try not to take his/her comments too seriously, as this is just part of his/her character trait. If you do take negative comments to your heart, it can create resentment and anger towards the other person, which could damage the relationship.

You should remember, people who criticise everything or make scathing remarks to be hurtful are the ones that need help, not you. If you are not critical, you will be liked by one and all and thus, you will gain confidence.

The key thing to remember is that whatever the circumstance is, don't respond in anger as this will cause a scene and create bad feelings, and possibly a bad image of you. You should try to remain calm and treat the other person with respect and understanding. This will help to defuse the situation and potentially stop it from getting out of hand.

You should show that you are the stronger person and try not to rise to the bait, do not use it as a reason to offer counter criticism. If you challenge the other person, you may start an argument that is probably unnecessary.

Sometime if you do feel that you may lose self-control, or say or do something potentially damaging, you should walk away. If you are in a meeting or at work, politely excuse yourself and leave the room until you have had time to gather yourself. Even though somebody's negative remarks may hurt you, it is more harmful for you to allow their criticism to be destructive to your confidence.

20. Take the Positives Out of Criticism

You should take Criticism wisely. We all learn by making mistakes, and learning how to deal with criticism positively is one way that you can improve our relationships with others.

You should remember that we all make mistakes all the time, it is human nature. As we go through life we have plenty of opportunity to learn and improve ourselves. Therefore, no matter what kind of criticism is aimed at you, analyse it to find something you can learn from it. When somebody is attacking your character it is hard to accept, but that does not mean you should ignore it or start fighting.

Also bear in mind that the criticism aimed at you may not make sense at the time. Generally speaking, there is usually some truth in criticism, even when it appears to be given out of bitterness. It is often the case that a slight on your character is a fair reflection of how another person sees you at that point in time.

You should take a step back and try to see things from the other person's point of view, perhaps ask a friend for his honest opinion. You should use criticism wisely and as a learning experience. See if it is possible to learn a little about how others perceive you, you may be able to use criticism to improve your interpersonal skills.

21. Try to be Polite

Being polite means being aware of and respecting the feelings of other people. We may not always notice politeness of others but we usually notice rudeness or inconsiderate behaviour of others.

Politeness can and will improve your relationships with others. It can also help to build respect and rapport, boost your self-esteem and confidence, and improve your communication skills.

It is easy to recognise when people are rude or inconsiderate but often more difficult to recognise these traits in yourself. Think carefully about the impressions you leave on others and how you can easily avoid being considered ill-mannered or ignorant.

22. Develop Your Interpersonal Communication Skills

First of all, let us explain what interpersonal communication is. Interpersonal communication is the process by which people exchange information, feelings, and meaning through verbal and non-verbal messages. You may say that it is face-to-face communication.

Interpersonal communication is not just about what is actually said, or the language used, but how it is said and the non-verbal messages sent through tone of voice, facial expressions, gestures and body language.

Without speech, an observer may be using cues of posture, facial expression, and dress to form an impression of the other's role, emotional state, personality and intentions. Although no communication may be intended, people receive messages through such forms of non-verbal behaviour also.

When two or more people are in the same place and are aware of each other's presence, then communication is taking place, no matter how subtle or unintentional. If you are expert in interpersonal communication skills, either you receive or send such communication, you feel confident about yourself.

23. Adopt a positive attitude of 'I can' or 'I shall'

Have you ever felt unmotivated or discouraged? Do you set goals in your mind and never attain these goals? Do you feel as if you are pessimistic and tend to think negatively at times? Here, are a few tips toward building positive attitude from the negative. A little advice will be provided on building your confidence and helping you become a better person. This will help you work to your full potential with a few simple daily tasks. Become the better person you deserve to be.

"Life is a challenge and a positive mind can make life's journey worth your time."

Follow the following tips-

1. Every morning, wake up and remind yourself of all your accomplishments and goals.

2. Positive Self-talk is very essential for confidence, you should more aware of your thoughts. Get into the habit of thinking positively. Tell yourself "you are the best," "you will achieve," "you can!," Get rid of all the fear and the negativity and simply replace it by these positive thoughts.

3. Set your daily goals and daily schedules and make sure to complete them. A list is very helpful and as you go about your day. You cross out each to do step on that list and before you feel it your day is over and you have succeeded. The fulfilment, you will experience as you cross out each step is priceless. Seeing your list slowly but surely disappearing is also satisfying and priceless.

4. You should be kind to yourself and to others.

5. You should remind yourself that you are a kind person, you are nice, you are helpful and you make a difference with each kind action you take and make.

6. You should constantly remind yourself of all the nice things you do for others. You can start with Simple things as simply saying "thank you" and "You are Welcome". Do any courteous gestures such as holding the door open or picking up an object for someone, helping an old lady cross the street. Practice positive and nice tiny gestures and you will notice that your self-esteem is feeling much better and fulfilled and you are developing confidence.

7. Don't ever let other's criticism, judgments and negativity get in your way or discourage you. On the contrary let the pessimists help motivate you into achieving and becoming the best person you can possibly be.

8. You can repeat to yourself "I am the best" "I am competent" I am confident" "I will" "I can" and "I am". Soon enough you will believe it and once you have believed it, you will then achieve it.

9. You should read inspirational books and articles such as books about successful people, peace of mind, self-discipline and will power. Knowledge is power and knowledge goes a long way. The more you learn the more you understand and the stronger your brain becomes and more confident you are.

10. You can listen to motivational music. You should stay away from negative people and negative music. Listen to music that uplifts your spirit and motivates you into becoming a better person, into becoming the best person.

11. You cannot change the fact that you have had some failures and setbacks throughout your life but you can change the way you perceive them and your perception on things is very crucial.

12. You should understand where and how you went wrong and come up with ways to make things better in the future, ways to help prevent repeating these same mistakes.

13. Instead of looking at the negative you should focus on all the many critical lessons you have learned throughout your negative experiences.The outcome of such negative situations is usually the lesson you learned.

24. Don't Compare Yourself to Others

Some people develop the bad habit of always comparing themselves to others. The problem with these comparisons is that they are usually triggered when people find that they are lacking something.

This means that people, who compare themselves again and again, attempt to play a game that they have already lost. If a guy was walking down the street and then saw some friend passing by with his pretty girlfriend his negative self talk will be triggered and he might start saying things like "I don't have a pretty girl friend like my friend like my friend, I feel that makes me less worthy than him, may be I am ugly or may be some other reason".

As you can see the comparison started when the guy already discovered that he has lost it. The comparison started because of one thing which is lack of self confidence.

This works like a self reinforcing cycle, you first feel that you are inferior and then you assume that you lack something compared to others. After words on finding anything that you miss, you start the comparison and so reinforce your false beliefs about yourself.

You should train yourself to stop comparing yourself to others to stop this cycle.

The second mistake people do when they start to compare themselves to others is choosing just one trait then making their whole judgment based on it. You should look at the whole matter comparing yourself to others. *For example,* a person may be very intelligent yet considers himself inadequate because he is not as good as his friends in playing cricket or hockey.

Therefore, if it's a must to compare yourself to someone else then compare the whole package and not just a single trait. Yes he may be more handsome than you but you may be smarter than him. He may be richer than you but you may be happier than him. Think of yourself as a package because it not fair to judge yourself based on only one thing that you don't have or that you can't do.

25. Don't Create Poor Self Image and Poor Body Image

Poor self-image affects your life and self-confidence. Many times you think that you are looking bad or too ugly or not attractive? Do you know the fact that many people think that they are ugly only because they have a poor self-image and not because they really look bad? Many people have images for themselves inside their minds that are much different than reality. This is called a self image problem.

As you meet a new person, you might start to think of your looks in the terms of the image that you have in your mind. So you think that the other person won't like you because you are bad looking while in reality your looks may be much different than this incorrect image.

You might think how was this poor self image built? Where did that incorrect image come from?

There may be many reasons. This image was most likely formed as a result of the criticism that you have received about your looks when you were a child. If you were always been called names such as fool, stupid when you were young then these words might turn into beliefs. In such a case you may associate this belief with your looks and so think you look like a fool.

When someone, who has a poor self-image, starts to ignore this problem and acts as if it's not there, he usually ends up with a severe depression. You should never take the risk of waiting and should do your best to solve this problem immediately.

In order to know if your beliefs about your looks are true or whether they are the result of your poor self image then ask your trust worthy person about it.

How to improve yourself image?

Try to think, you experience any moment where you thought that you are good looking? If you have found that one day you felt that you are good looking or that at least you have above average looks, it means probably your beliefs about your looks are the result of your poor mental self-image and not because of looking bad in real life.

You have to understand that you be may be looking fine but it's just a poor mental self-image that you have in your mind that makes you think that you are looking bad.

You don't have to suffer in order to have a perfect body; you just need to know about more powerful techniques that are based on psychology instead of the motivational advice found everywhere.

26. Take Risks and Action to Build Confidence

Wise people say –

"If you always do what you've always done, then you'll always get what you've already got."

If you want major change in your life and want to develop absolute confidence, you must change those self-limiting beliefs that have kept you from having what you've wanted in the past.

The fact is that you are always taking risks in your life. If you drive your car, or get on a ship or plane, or cross a street or go to market anything you do, you're taking a risk. You can also choose what kind of risk you take. So why not choose ones that are in your best interest?

All confident people share one common trait, they take risks and take action. To be confident, you should get out there and try new things.

You should learn a new skill or try a new hobby. Don't be worried about failure or rejection. Failure is an opportunity to learn and grow. If it didn't work out, figure out why, make some changes and try it again. If you take a risk and you are not successful, you can take pride in knowing that at least you gave it a try and learned something new.

You can change your life and gain self confidence by taking risks in your life. To start you can do following things-

1. Start by taking small risks. The more risks you take, the

easier it gets.

2. Don't over-think taking a risk. Just do it. The easiest way to get into a cold swimming pool is to jump right in.

3. Act in-spite of your fears.

4. Ask yourself, "What do I have to lose?" There's usually nothing to lose! It's more about your ego.

5. At times be first to do things. Have the courage to try something before waiting to see if others will.

6. After taking risk and getting success you can reward yourself.

27. Enjoy what you do and do what you enjoy

In your life if you enjoy what you do, this feeling gives you confidence. If you do thing what you enjoy, you feel more confident about it.

You enjoy doing things that challenge you sufficiently, yet are instructive to you, that engage you. For instance, selling to a difficult customer may be you're hobby. It may be engaging to you for your own reason, some others may hate the same tasks.

A career means different things to different people. To some, it is an end point, to some it may be an ambition. For instance, I must become the CEO of this company. To others, it means the landmarks on the way; I must become regional manager in two years and GM in three years thereafter. To most people, it is a combination. But, these are all 'destinations' and not the 'journey' for confident persons.

To wise persons, it means the enjoyment and experiences of work. A career is not a destination, it is the journey. So what kind of a journey should you have? The answer is, 'a journey which you enjoy'. You can excel with consistency only at tasks that you enjoy. In the some way you cannot excel with consistency at tasks that you do not enjoy. Enjoyment does not mean that the task is easy, or that you know how to do it. It is a matter of interest and confidence. If you enjoy your tasks, you will surely develop confidence.

28. Try To Overcome Self-Doubt to Boost Your Confidence

At one point or another, we all questions whether or not we are doing enough, making enough money, or if we are going to be "successful" enough. You know this very well, as you have spent long periods of your young adult life in a persistent state of fear and self-doubt.

You can remember that you doubted yourself to the point that you were making your decisions based on what others wanted of you and not what you wanted for yourself. You were constantly struggling with confidence and always guessing yourself.

You should learn that if you don't nip the self-limiting thoughts in the bud right away, this "self doubt" mindset can become painful. You should know a few things to help with self-doubt and boost your confidence that may help you:

1. You should stop comparing your accomplishments to your friends' and colleagues' accomplishments.Your colleague's accomplishments are not a litmus test to grade your own success.

One important thing to remember, when you find yourself in this mental pattern, is that everyone is on his or her own journey.

You will find that you are most successful in your personal and professional life when you are following what works for you and what makes you feel good, even if it is different from what someone you look up to is doing.

2. Just make a decision and then correct your course as you go along.

A specialist says, "no feeling is final" and the same could be said about your decisions. Just make a decision, and then fine-tune your course along the way.

Getting caught up in a decision is another sure way to water the seeds of self-doubt. It's very easy to get stuck in trying to make decisions. This back-and-forth thought process and questioning if you should go with option A or option B, can exacerbate your self-doubt.

3. You must forget about what everyone else is thinking of you.

Worrying about what other people think of you will continue to hold you back from doing something potentially huge for yourself. When you care about what everyone else is thinking of you, you inhibit yourself. You'd rather do nothing and not get judged, than do something and face criticism.

If you hold your own dreams for your future, which you probably do, then at some point you have to let go of everyone else's opinion. Otherwise, you'll find yourself in a constant state of self-doubt.

4. You should listen and read positive material on a daily basis.

One of your quick trial ways to boost your confidence is to listen to some music and read some of your favourite self-development books.

5. You can write yourself a hand-written letter.

Sometimes a kind word or compliment from someone can totally bring you out of a slump. But what if you're feeling low and unconfident and no one is around to pick you up? Well, there will always be one person left to uplift you and that's you yourself. A great exercise is writing yourself a hand-written letter.

This negative, doubtful, scared part of yourself is your shadow side and you all have one. And just as you have a shadow, you also have a light side, the positive, optimistic and productive self, to improve yourself.

6. You should identify your biggest friends and nurture those relationships.

No man or woman is all alone, that means, you can't do it all on your own. Sometimes all you need is a little reassurance and your biggest friends are the people who think and do just for you.

You first need to identify your biggest friends and close persons. They may be friends, family members, and peers who have always been there for you. Friends are those who tell you that you're awesome.

Then, put your energy into fostering deeper and lasting relationships with these people. You all have them, so nurture those relationships and draw strength and confidence from them.

7. You can write your feeling of gratitude at the end of each day.

Feelings of gratitude put you in a positive frame of mind. When you're feeling positive, you're feeling good. And when you're feeling good, good things happen.

Instead of focusing on what you are lacking, focus on what you do have and what you have accomplished. This fosters a feeling of gratitude, and when you invest energy into gratitude now, you will start to find that you will be rewarded in the future.

29. Set your goals and work Toward them

If you are setting your goals and working towards them, it can help you turn your dreams into reality. Goals are things you set to accomplish either in a long period of time or a short period of time.

You can have two types of goals.

1. Short Term Goals:

These are goals that you can accomplish within a short period of time, like 2-3 days or 2 weeks.

2. Long Term Goals:

These are goals that you can accomplish within a long period of time, like 6 months or 1 to 5 years.

You can follow these steps to set and work towards your goals:

Step 1: You should be clear on the outcome you want to achieve. The more defined your vision, the easier it will be set goals and objectives. This will also help you stay focused on the things that will help you achieve your goals easily.

Step 2: You should write down your goals. Take time to write out all the goals you have for yourself. If you have personal and business goals, write them out separately. You may wish to work on one area at a time so that you do not become overwhelmed and mix your goal. People are often unable to achieve goals because they become overwhelmed with the tasks and feel they will not be able to accomplish them all. If you break goals into smaller areas, chances of success increase.

Step 3: Put your goals and objectives into time frames. Look at your overall list and figure out what goals need to be accomplished first for you to achieve larger goals. You can breakdown your goals into 3 month, 6 month, 1 year, and 5 year time frames.

Step 4: You should determine the objectives for each goal. Objectives break each goal down into smaller steps. By working on one step at a time, you are able to achieve your goals more easily and there is more clarity about the tasks you are undertaking.

Step 5: You should review your goals. Read each goal and objective and visualize what it will feel like to achieve it. The more you can visualize the more real it will become to you. At this step, it may be a good idea if you create a vision board with pictures of the goals. These pictures can help motivate you to stay on track to achieve your goals.

Step 6: You should put your list in a place that is easily accessible. You should have a copy on your computer or carry a copy with you in a goals and objectives notebook. It is a good idea if you wish to write in it daily or when you accomplish a goal.

Step 7: You should return to your lists after each time frame. You should take time to sit and review what goals and objectives you were able to reach and which ones you missed. If you were not able to accomplish some goals, think of what steps you could take differently to accomplish them and set goals again for that task.

30. Set Realistic Expectations

Nothing can kill your self-confidence more than setting unrealistic expectations. Here, is an example. When Sandeep was in his 20s, he had thought, "I need to be a millionaire by the time I'm 30 or I'm going to be a failure." Needless to say, 30 came and he was nowhere close to being a millionaire. He was more in debt than ever and owning a home was still a distant dream. His expectation was unrealistic and his self-confidence took a blow when he turned 30 and saw how far away such a goal was.

Sometimes your expectations are so much smaller, but still unrealistic. For instance, "You wish your mom or dad or sister would stop criticizing you." Guess what? They never will! But that's no reason to let their criticism affect your own view of yourself, or your own self-worth. Check your expectations if they keep disappointing you.

This may also help you to stop the cycle of negative thinking about yourself that reinforce your negative self-esteem and self-confidence. When you make set realistic expectations in your life, you can stop criticizing yourself for not meeting some idealistic goals.

31. Explore Yourself and know your capability

"Know yourself" is an old saying passed down through the ages, to encourage us to engage in self-exploration. It is not just about knowing your strengths and weaknesses, but also opening yourself up to new opportunities, new thoughts, trying out something new, new viewpoints, and new friendships. Usually the most well-adjusted and happiest people are people who have gone through this exploration.

Sometimes when you are down on yourself and your self-confidence takes a big hit. You feel like you have nothing to offer the world or others. It may be that you simply have not found everything that you do have to offer. Learning what these are, is simply a matter of trial and error. It's how people become the people they've always wanted to become, by taking risks and trying things they wouldn't ordinarily do.

32. Set Aside Perfection

You should Set aside perfection and grab a hold of accomplishment and mistakes.

Perfection is simply unattainable for any of us. Let it go. You are never going to be perfect. You are never going to have the perfect body, the perfect life, the perfect relationship, the perfect children, or the perfect home. You believe in the idea of perfection, because you see so much of it in the media. But that is simply an artificial creation of society. It doesn't exist.

Instead, you should grab a hold of your accomplishments as you achieve them. Acknowledge them to yourself for their actual value. Don't de-value them by saying, "Oh, that? That's just so easy for me, no big deal." It may even help to keep a little list of things you accomplish. Some people might even do this on a day-by-day basis, while others might feel more comfortable just noting them once a week or even once a month. The key is to get to your smaller goals and move on from each one, like a connect-the-dots game of life. Your accomplishments develop a sense of self confidence in you.

It's important to learn from the mistakes you make in life. It doesn't mean you're a bad person, it simply means you made a mistake, like everyone does in life. Mistakes are an opportunity for learning and for growth. You should push yourself out of the self-pity or negative self-talk. Generally you try and see it from someone else's eyes.

33. Take Good Care of Yourself

Another way you can build your self-confidence is to take very good care of yourself. You may take very good care of others and put your own personal care last. Your life may be so busy that you don't take the time to do the things you need to do to stay healthy. Sometimes you may feel so badly about yourself that you don't bother to take good care of yourself.

Some of the things you can do to take good care of your health and yourself include:

- You can avoid foods that contain large amounts of sugar, caffeine and food additives. If you can't pronounce the ingredients, you may want to avoid it.
- Eating three meals a day that are focused on healthy foods—fresh fruit and vegetables, as well as whole grain foods and rich sources of protein like chicken and fish if you like.
- Getting outside and exercising every day.
- Spending time each day with people who make you feel good about yourself.
- Spending some time each day doing something you really enjoy.
- Having regular check-ups with your health care advisers and doctors.

34. Change Negative Thoughts about Yourself to Positive Ones

Do hard work on changing negative thoughts about yourself to positive ones. You may give yourself lots of negative self talk. Many people do. This negative self talk worsens your self-confidence. You can decide now not to do this to yourself. That's great if you can do it. However, negative self talk is often a habit that is hard to break. You may need to work on it more directly by changing negative statements about yourself to positive ones. Begin this process by making a list of the negative statements you often say to yourself. Some of the most common negative thoughts are:

- I never do anything right.
- Nobody likes me.
- I am ugly.
- I'm not worth anything.
- I've never accomplished anything worthwhile.
- Everyone is better than I am.
- I am dumb.
- I am a failure.

Develop a positive statement that refutes the negative one. For instance, instead of saying to yourself, "Nobody likes me" you could say, "Many people like me". You could even make a list of the people who like you. Instead of saying, "I am ugly", you could say "I look fine". Instead of saying, "I never do anything right" you could say "I have done many things right." You could even make a list of things you have done right. It helps to do this work in a special notebook. You can read the notebook, when there is need to do so.

When you have developed positive statements that refute your negative statements, read them before you go to bed at night and when you first get up in the morning. Read them aloud to your partner, a close friend or your advisor. Make signs that say a positive statement about you and post them where you will see them like on the mirror in your bathroom. Read them aloud every time you see them.

35. Make a List of Your Accomplishments

You may not give yourself credit for all that you have achieved in your life. Making a list of your accomplishments will help you become more aware of these accomplishments. It will also help change the focus of your self-thoughts to positive ones. You can do this exercise again and again, whenever you notice your self-confidence is low.

Get a big sheet of paper and a comfortable pen. Spend the time writing your accomplishments. You could never have a paper long enough or enough time to write them all. This list can include even small things which you do every day and you want for will do today like-

- Making and keeping a good friend
- Planting some seeds or caring for houseplants
- Raising a child
- Driving your car or catching the subway
- Buying your groceries
- Making the bed
- Making the dishes
- Getting a job
- Smiling at a person who looks sad
- Taking a difficult course
- Dealing with a major illness or disability
- Learning to talk, walk, read, skip

Watch for opportunities that come up every day. You can buy your partner some flowers or even one rose for your partner. Send a friend a greeting card. If someone you know is having a hard time, send them a note or give them a call. Go out of your way to congratulate people you know on their achievements. Visit a patient at a nursing home or hospital or someone who is "shut-in." Play with a child-read him a book, take him/her for a walk, push him on the swing. Do a chore for someone that might be hard for her or him like collecting the leaves, plucking the flower or mowing the grass. You may even want to volunteer for an organization that is helping others, like a heart association or old age home project. You can think of many other ideas.

Have you ever noticed the good feeling that washes over you when you do something nice for someone else? If so, take advantage of that good feeling by doing things that are "nice" or helpful to others as often as you can to build your self-confidence.

36. Motivate yourself to Get Something Done

Low self-confidence is often accompanied with lack of motivation. It may feel very hard to do anything. Motivation will help you to feel better about yourself if you do something, even if it is a very small thing. You may want to keep a list of possibilities on hand for those times when you can't think of anything to do. You can do many things like: cleaning out one drawer, washing the outside of your refrigerator, putting a few pictures in a photo album, reading an article, you have been wanting to read, taking a picture of a beautiful flower or a person you love, making the bed, doing a load of laundry, cooking yourself something healthy, sending someone a card, hanging a picture or taking a short walk. This will give you satisfaction of doing something nice, you will step towards.

37. Take action to Get it done

Having once decided to achieve a certain task, achieve it at all costs of your hard work. The gain of self-confidence after having accomplished a tiresome work is immense. Nothing builds self-esteem and self-confidence like accomplishment.

The most important step in building self-confidence is simply to take action, working on something and getting it done. Sitting at home and thinking about it will just make you feel bitter. But it is not always easy to do a work. Here, are a three ways to make it easier to take action:

1. **You should fell yourself light and easy-**

One way to dissuade yourself from taking action is to take whatever you are about to do too seriously. That makes it feel too big, too difficult and too scary. If you on the other hand relax a bit and lighten up you often realize that those problems and negative feelings are just nothing you are creating in your own mind. With a lighter state of mind your tasks seems lighter and become easier to get started with.

2. **You should be present at your work-**

This will help you snap out of over thinking and just go and do whatever you want to get done. One of the simplest ways to connect with the present moment is just to keep your focus on your breathing for a minute or two.

3. **Have the feeling that you really want to do it-**

Then taking action isn't something you have to force.

Taking action becomes a very natural thing. It's something you can't wait to do.

It is rightly said-

"Inaction breeds doubt and fear. Action breeds confidence and courage. If you want to conquer fear, do not sit home and think about it. Go out and get busy."

38. Realise that failure or bring wrong will not kill you

"I quit being afraid when my first venture failed and the sky didn't fall down."

"Confidence comes not from always being right but from not fearing to be wrong"

It is truly said by an expert.

Again, you have to face your fear for being wrong. Because it is only then that you discover the thing that billions of people throughout history have discovered before you. Failure won't kill you. The sky will not fall down. That's what people have faced their fear.

The thing is to reframe failure from being something that makes your legs shake to something useful and important for the growth of your self-confidence and your overall growth as a human being.

Here, are the ways that failure can help you out:

- You gain experiences with your failures that you could not get any other way. Ideally, you would probably want to learn from other people's mistakes and failures. That's not always easy to do so. Sometimes you just have to fail on your own to learn a lesson and to gain an experience.

- When you make a mistake actually, you learn. Instead of seeing failure as something horrible you can start to view it more as a learning experience. When standing in the middle of a failure, you can ask yourself questions like: What can I learn from this situation?

- Your chances of success increase with failure. Every time you fail you can learn and increase your inner strength. So every failure can make you more and more likely to succeed.

- You become stronger after failure. Every time you fail, you realize that it's not the end of the world. And, again, you get courage to work hard. You can handle things that would have been very hard to handle a few years back. Failing can also a have an exhilarating component because even though you failed, you at least took a chance. You feel that you didn't just sit on your hands doing nothing and that took quite a bit of your courage and determination.

You should remember that the world doesn't revolve around you. You may like to think so. But it doesn't. People really don't care that much about what you do. They have their own life, problems and worries to focus on. They don't think that much about you or are constantly monitoring what you do wrong or when you fail. So try to learn a lesson from your failure to gain confidence.

It may be a disappointing thought. But this is a relieving thought because now you can let go of that worry that everyone is watching your mistakes.

39. Know yourself better

Don't listen to anyone who tells you that you can't do this or that. That's nonsense. Make up your mind. Go to school; join in all the games you can. Go anywhere you want to. But never let them persuade you that things are too difficult or impossible.

You have to know who you are and what you want out of life. To build and find more confidence in yourself you have to get to know yourself better. You should go exploring. Face some of your fears. Fail over and over and understand that it isn't really that big of a deal. Grow stronger through such experiences and also become more internally relaxed. Figure out what really excites you.

When you know more about yourself, who you are and what you want out of life – not other people tell what they want, you will have more confidence in yourself about what you can do.

What other people say or think will have less of an impact than it used. And since you have had all these experiences and since you have taken time to really get to know yourself, stretch yourself you will trust your own opinion and ability more than anyone outside of you. You become stable and centred in yourself. This will of course take time. It may be something that never really ends.

"The world has the habit of making room for the man whose words and actions show that he knows where he is going."-Napoleon.

40. Some Quick Things You Can Do to Raise Your Self-Esteem

Following is a list of other things you can do to raise your self-esteem. Some of them will be right at one time, while others will work at another time. There may be some you choose not to do ever. You may like to post this list in your diary, bathroom or at some other convenient place as a reminder.

- Does something that makes you laugh?
- Pretend you are your own best friend.
- Make a collage of your life.
- Wear something that makes you feel good.
- Repeat positive statements over and over again.
- Spend 10 minutes writing down everything good you can think of about yourself.
- Look through old pictures, scrapbooks and photo albums.
- Surround yourself with people who are positive, affirming and loving.

You can add more ideas to this list as you discover them for yourself and you will develop a sense of confidence.

41. Have Social Confidence And Overcome You Fears And Self Doubts

There are many powerful techniques used by psychologists and life coaches to help you overcome your fears and self-doubts. Whatever area your lack of confidence is impacting, you should know some basic, easily applicable tools and strategies you can start using to know the trusts.

First of all "You should change how you think and feel about yourself". As you change the way you think about yourself, you can feel more confident and enjoy the success you truly desire in your life.

It is always possible to believe in yourself and to have the courage to be who you are in any situation. You should have trust that you're capable of achieving your dreams!

You should to find, Are you struggling with any of the following:-

- You feel tense or awkward during conversations and struggle to find things to say.
- You feel nervous and uncomfortable before meeting new people.
- You feel an intense fear of starting conversations with attractive women.
- You have a hard time speaking up at work and are often quiet in meetings. Co-workers and supervisors don't seem to respect your opinion or appreciate your talents.
- You have difficulty asking women out and often find

yourself being just a friend.

- You hate putting yourself out there in a group and being the centre of attention.
- You feel embarrassed and self-critical afterwards, wishing you'd been different.

You should try to find the solution by doing the following:-

- Overcome your fear of rejection.
- Feel more comfortable when meeting new people.
- Realize your strengths and increase your self-esteem.

By following these things you will also learn the one essential thing you must do in order to build true self-confidence *i.e* believe in yourself. No matter what your situation is, it's possible for you to feel more confident in yourself.

42. Access The power of your sub-conscious Mind

Low self-esteem is a result of the sub-conscious mind being fed with negative and defeating beliefs such as: I can't, I'm useless, I will never do it, nobody likes me, I'm so angry, I'm so depressed etc. The sub-conscious mind is all powerful; it is working while you are asleep and awake. It is designed for all to lead satisfying lives and has been responsible for the great creations of mankind.

However, you struggling in your day-to-day lives, have not come to understand how you can use it for its good. The sub-conscious mind is amazing in ensuring your well being in body, mind and soul. It is responsible for all unconscious processes such as heart beat and hair growth. It heals your wounds,reproduces your cells and grants you unlimited creativity.

Most people go through life without having any knowledge of an amazing intelligence born with as a precious gift. It allows them to use their minds to create what they want.

Your conscious mind is involved in processing your conscious thoughts through your sensory perceptive systems. Whatever you touch, feel, smell, taste, see, or hear will be processed through your conscious minds. So while eating a favourite food you are consciously aware that the food tastes nice and you begin to tell your sub-conscious mind how wonderful the food is by continually affirming it verbally and through taste and smell. Whatever you continue to tell your sub-conscious mind, your sub-conscious mind will digest and make truth of. So, in simple terms, one sure way to increase self-esteem which has been proven to work is to continually practice verbal affirmations which lead your sub-conscious minds into happiness.

Here, is the key to improving self-esteem through the sub-conscious mind. You can personalize it to your own needs, practice the exercise daily, twice daily, or thrice daily and notice great results:

1. Find a quiet place to relax alone, a comfortable space where you are not likely to be disturbed. Please do not try this exercise while driving or operating any machinery or doing any difficult task.

2. Focus on your breathing. Breathe through the diaphragm by pumping your tummy out like a balloon as you breathe in, holding it for five seconds, then breathing out again, do this continuously for 5-10 minutes.

3. Sit or lie comfortably and if possible. You can set the place with some nice quiet relaxation music.

4. Repeat the following words "I'm feeling good, I feel relaxed, I like myself in all situations". Repeat this ten times.

5. Visualize being on a nice beach with sunshine or at a mountain and notice how relaxed you are. Be aware still of your breathing and its calming effect on your body.

6. Repeat the following words "My joy is within me, I like myself in every way, I'm strong".

You should always remember the infinite wisdom of the sub-conscious mind is a source of divine energy which can be tapped into at any time. You should always feed your subconscious mind with positive healthy thoughts by affirming positive phrases. Likewise create nice vivid images in your mind of beautiful scenes, look regularly at sunsets, clouds, trees, and lakes or rivers. These images are great for the mind. To have peace you should set yourself towards great confidence.

43. Try to Practice the Art of Good Deeds

"Goodness Is The Only Investment That Never Fails".

The practice of the art of good deeds makes you more confident. Many of people lose the idea of feeling good about them, because they lead busy demanding lifestyles.

You are often so busy doing things for others that you end up feeling unappreciated. Sometimes you are busy trying to meet a deadline or finish a project that you lose valuable time with family and friends. Then there are some of us, who are so burdened with current worries, problems and setbacks, that we seem to lack in appreciation of ourselves and who you really are.

Self-esteem can reach different points in different areas of your life and is a very internal concept. You might try hard to create an image of yourself as having great esteem, when really inside you are aware of quite the contrary.

If you want to start feeling good in your life, you should start by inwardly creating some good things you can do in every area of your life. You can act on these ideas: -

1. Take a bag of goods to a local charity shop and don't tell anyone about this

2. Pick litter up on the local play area where your child plays regularly

3. Exchange greetings with a stranger, comment on what a beautiful day it is

4. Give a friend or colleague a compliment on how well he looks today. You should really mean it

5. Congratulate the next door neighbour who just found a job or he got admission in a professional course

6. Smile at passerby who you find particularly attractive

The idea is for you to recognize that you can incorporate small and simple things into your own life, to create inner feelings of self-worth. It can be as simple as offering a warm smile to your neighbour, thanking a shopkeeper for a kind service, or picking up the phone and telling a distant relative that you miss him. You can start now creating goodness and enjoy the results. You should remember to tap into your sub-conscious mind, by becoming relaxed and asking it to provide you with the means to create new ideas to do 'good' things in life.

44. Develop an Attitude of Gratitude

It is truly said. "To speak gratitude is courteous and pleasant, to enact gratitude is generous and noble but to live gratitude is to touch heaven."

You should ask yourself the question "How grateful am I ?" and then listen to yourself being as truthful as you can. Try to write down ten things you really have to be grateful for. These could be things from the past or the present. Is it easy for you to do this exercise? Did you struggle consciously recollecting them?

Gratitude and being thankful for what we have, what we love, They may be our special gifts materially, is a positive attitude which has an amazing effect on our self-esteem and self-confidence. Important matter is, you do have something to be grateful.

When you decide to be grateful for the things you have, you are making a conscious decision to appreciate these things. This immediately evokes a sense of joy and contentment which will add to your measure of self esteem and confidence. Many of us take for granted the beauty of a day, the blessing of good health, strengths and attributes, loved ones, material possessions, and feel free to choose our own life path.

Being grateful about the little things in your life is the start to creating a greater sense of inner gratitude which will lead to greater self-esteem. To many, it will seem like an unusual concept, to some it will seem abnormal. Many choose to be ungrateful and meet with frustration, want, and discontentment.

Be grateful for the small things, a friendly greeting from a stranger, the peace of a nice quiet place, a new person who has come into your life.

- Think about a difficult time when you were unsure how things were going to pan out. A time where you felt all alone. Be grateful for the fact you came through it and the strength you have now gained as a result.
- "To speak gratitude is courteous and pleasant, to enact gratitude is generous and noble, but to live gratitude is to touch heaven", a wise saying says so.

45. Lead a life of laughter

"Laughter is the best medicine" a proverb says.

Laughter has a great impact on our self-esteem levels. Some of us move within social circles where laughter is common place. Laughter is undoubtedly healthy and scientists have proven that laughter is linked to happiness. Laughter can create great happiness in people.

How much laughter do you have in your life at present?

Carry with you a small note pad and record how many times a day laugh. Be your own researcher and act as your own laughter consultant. Do you have a favourite comedian or comedy actor? If so, start to watch more films/programmes with your favourite comedy actor. Do you watch much television where deceit and hatred are the drama? Instead, you should explore when you can watch pure comedy shows which are your preferential choice.

Think, you are an amazing person and once you come to understand that you can control all aspects of your life, you will start to notice better levels of self-esteem. Control your ability to increase the amount of fun you have. The more childlike you can be, the more creative you can be.

Children are always laughing as they are innocent to the negative ways of the world. They are seldom interested in international conflicts, local newspaper headlines which promote fear, or general negativity. Children can teach adults lots about the way we could improve our lives.

Learn to laugh more. Laughter is an instant vacation from fears and sorrows. Laughter is universal, it is custom to all nationalities. Laughter brings us hope and happiness. Thus, there comes self-confidence.

46. Stay Calm To Gain Confidence

You ability to manage your emotions and remain calm under pressure has a direct link to your performance. You will see that top performers are skilled at managing their emotions in times of stress in order to remain calm and in control.

The tricky thing about stress is that it's an absolutely necessary emotion. Our brains are wired such that it's difficult to take action until we feel at least some level of this emotional state. In fact as long as the stress isn't prolonged, it's harmless.

Confident persons avoid asking "What if?" Such statements throw fuel on the fire of stress and worry. Things can go in a million different directions, and the more time you spend worrying about the possibilities, the less time you'll spend focusing on taking action that will calm you down and keep your stress under control. Calm and confident people know that asking "what if? Will only take them to a place they don't want – or need – to go.

47. Think Positive

When things are going well and your mood is good, this is relatively easy to think positive. When things are going poorly and your mind is flooded with negative thoughts, this can be a challenge. In these moments, think about your day and identify one positive thing that happened recently or in past, no matter how small.

Positive thoughts help make stress intermittent by focusing your brain's attention onto something that is completely stress-free. You have to give your wandering brain a little help by consciously selecting something positive to think about. Any positive thought will refocus your attention and you will feel confidence about your next step of work.

If you can't think of something from the current day, reflect on the previous day or even the previous week. You can look forward to an exciting event that you can focus your attention on. The point here is that you must have something positive that you are ready to shift your attention to when your thoughts turn negative.

48. Try to Be Friendly

Being friendly is all about making people feel comfortable in your orbit. Friendly people are excited to meet new people. They appear approachable to friends and acquaintances and are the kind of people who can just start chatting up a person in a train, in line at the booking movie ticket, or when they're stuck on the bus. Does this sound hard? It doesn't have to be, if you are friendly with the people around you. It's true that you will feel very confident about yourself. To learn to be friendly try the following things –

1. A way to be friendlier is to notice everything that's going on around you instead of trying to beat the new level of Candy Crush on your Mobile Phone. If you're tapping away at your phone or reading a book or staring at your computer, or even just looking at the paint of your fingernails, then people will think you have better things to do than to talk to them. Instead, you should look ahead, smile and be ready for what the other person has to offer you. You'll be surprised by how many more people will be friendly and how quickly they come your way.

2. You should try to smile more. However, making a goal to smile at least 30% more on a daily basis, whether you're smiling at people you know, complete strangers, or acquaintances that cross your path, will make you look like a much more approachable, friendly person. Remember when you passed that person you met that one time and he looked in the other direction and pretended you didn't exist? How did that make you feel? If you want people to feel good about talking to you, then you should smile more at them.

3. Your ability to laugh easily is another trait of the friendly person. You don't have to laugh at everything a person says otherwise you may sound fake, But you should make an effort to laugh especially when people are trying to be funny. Laughing more will not only give your conversations more of a positive vibe, but the people around you will see you as a friendlier person.

4. You should make eye contact to be friendly. This is something you should work on whether you're just saying Hi. Say hello instead of staring at the floor or pretending to be fascinated by your own fingernails. You don't have to stare into a person's eyes 100% of the time to be friendly, but you should work on making as much eye contact as possible with people you're talking to so that they feel like you care about them and that they're actually worth your time.

To be more friendly remember the following things –

- Don't be shy. Say hello to people you haven't talked to in a while. Just keep in touch; it will be appreciated.
- Be yourself; don't be ashamed of who you are and

always give a friendly smile to people.

- Make a conscious decision to like people you meet. It will produce positive verbal and body language that will bring the best out of people.
- Look at yourself in the mirror and think positive thoughts about your appearance. If you like yourself, others will too.
- Always be polite!
- Everyone has something they really love, may be it a hobby, a pet, or a book. Try to find out what others love and take note of it.
- Never be rude or insulting to others.
- Never tell anyone your problems. Long after you've resolved your issues, others will remember your capability and appreciate you.
- Try to use people's names. A hint for remembering names is to repeat their name every time you see the person.

If you want people to feel like you're approachable and open to talking to them, then you have to master your body language. Here, are the things that you can do to make people want to talk to you more:

- Lean forward toward other people
- Have good posture instead of slouching
- Keep your arms at your sides instead of crossing them
- Keep your legs together instead of crossed.

49. Learn Traits Of Successful Conversation

If you want to be friendly and want to master your conversation, you have to show a real interest in people. They have to see that you really care about who they are, what they think and what they do. You shouldn't ask anything too personal or they might get offended. Here are some great topics you can try:-

- Favourite hobbies,
- Siblings,
- Weekend trips,
- Favourite bands, books, or movies,
- School or work,
- Favourite sports teams,
- Pets,

If you want to be confident about yourself learn the traits of mastering friendly conversation. You can do the following thing–

Have small talk:

Some people think that small talk is completely superficial, but it's not. All good friendships and relationships start out with a bit of small talk. You can even make small talk just to be nice. Make a comment about the weather or compliment that person's jewellery or dress. It'll make you feel more positiveand it'll make your day go by faster. Knowing how to make small talk will go a long way in making you friendlier. All you have to do is make the person feel comfortable, find some common ground and reveal a little bit about yourself.

Try to Compliment others:

Complimenting people will make you see and feel like a much more friendly and confident person. Just a small compliment given at the right time will make people think, "He's really nice!" and will make them feel more comfortable and happy to be in your presence.

Don't be rude:

You should know when you're giving people the cold shoulder. Some people are unfriendly without even realizing it. If someone has given you a big "Hi!" and is approaching you while slowing down, this is because that person wants to talk to you; if you just say "hey," and keep walking, then you'll look rude. You may think that you're just giving off a neutral or a busy vibe, but that may often come off as unfriendly behaviour.

Befriend people of your age and stage:

You should try to be friendly with you people. *For example,* if you're a young mother, join a young mothers group and you'll be on the way to making some amazing new friends. Finding people who are around your age and your stage will make you more likely to find time to hang out and will give you more things to talk about. A stage of life could be being a college student, being a young professional, being a middle-aged mother, or being an older person who spends more time alone.

Try to overcome your insecurities:

If you're lacking confidence and think that people will judge you any time you open your mouth. You can ask yourself what lies behind your distrust or coldness to other people and see if it has to do more with what you think of yourself. If that's the case, then work on loving the person who you are loving what you do and addressing the flaws that need some work. Of course, overcoming your insecurities can take years of hard work, but recognizing this as one of the sources of your problem with being friendly can make you be more willing to be nice to others. You should remember that they may be just as insecure as you are.

50. Make More Friends

Making more friends can make you confident person. You should chat back to people who try to talk to you. If someone is trying to chat with you, make an effort to give them something back in return. Have you ever tried making pleasant conversation with someone you've run into and they blew you off by giving one-word responses and obviously looking like they don't want to be spoken too? You probably walked away thinking they were pretty unfriendly.

Here, are ways to make friends. If you have lot of friends, than sure you will be very confident.

Start conversations with new people. If you've recently been introduced to someone, or you see some new people around, go up to them and start a conversation. Even saying Hi, asking for their name, and going, "Cool, nice meeting you. I'll see you around later hopefully" can be good. In this style you can make more friends.

Invite people to do things with you Be fairly loose and generous with your invitations to people. Be the one to invite people out rather than waiting for them to come to you first. Don't feel you have to know someone for a long time either. If you seem to get along them why not ask them to do something? If you like your new co-worker or classmate, ask his/her if he want to come by your place to chill. If you're meeting some friends later that night, ask your new acquaintance if he want to join you.

Take time to talk to people you already know. Keep in touch with your friends. Stop and chat to your co-workers when they're not too busy. Maintain your relationships and show you're interested in the other people.

Spend time with the people – Where you are. If you're at work and everyone is going out for lunch then go as well. If they all eat lunch at a certain time and place, then eat lunch then too. If you're at a party and everyone is talking on the front porch, go join them. Show you want to spend time with the people you come with. And once you're there, join in whatever they're doing. Don't hang back and focus on something else.

Offer compliments to people – Don't be afraid to be positive and encouraging. If someone is good at something then tell them so. Moderation is essential. The occasional genuine compliment is nice way to make friends.

You can make an effort to bring new people into the fold. When you make such effort, make them feel included. If you're out with your long-time friends and there's a new person there, take the time to talk to him/her a bit, rather than making him more aloof and expecting him/her to make the effort of getting to know you. Make nice little gestures towards other people. Bring food or drinks to a party when it wasn't expected that you do so. You should perform basic courtesies like holding doors for people. Buy someone a drink or a shot if you're out at a bar. However, less is more. But remember if you're overly "nice" and giving, you can be taken for granted, taken advantage of, or come across as if you're trying too hard to please everyone and make them like you.

51. Learn To Control Your Anger

You should learn to manage your feelings for better health. Most of the time you do not choose to be angry, but somehow you are suddenly in the feelings of anger. Often, you don't know we are angry until you feel it.

You may have noticed that what 'triggers' your anger one time may not do so at another time. Different people may also react very differently to the same event. Some people recover much more quickly than others when provoked by any negative emotion, including anger.

Angry feelings are a natural reaction to frustration or interference with our goals. Yet, we all are different in terms of what events trigger anger in us, how strongly we respond and how long it takes us to get back to normal. Learning to see a situation differently, cooling off and looking for alternative responses are all effective ways to better cope with angry feelings.

If you are a quick-recovering person, you probably are also better able to control your emotions. However, if you are challenged in this regard, you will need to work harder to develop anger management skills to deal with your feelings.

Anger, which comes from a part of your brain that is very old, can be very brief, lasting only a second or two. You can be happy one moment and angry the next. Angry feelings may also continue over a long period of time. If you are angry a lot, but your feelings are not connected to life circumstances, we call it a 'mood.' Angry moods lead to angry feelings coming on stronger and faster.

Once anger begins, it generates changes in your expression, your face, your voice and changes in the way you think. It also creates impulses to action. Sometimes you have thoughts that generate anger. Other times you have thoughts that occur at the same time as the anger. It is also possible for your anger to generate thoughts about what you are angry toward.

Suppose you are standing in the queue for railway ticket. You see that the person ahead of you is talking to the booking manager and asking absurd questions. The cashier is doing nothing to manage the situation and, in fact, is having a friendly chat with him about his life while other people are waiting in the line on that hot day.

If you are like most people, you will probably experience angry feelings. Then what should you do? How should you respond?

There are ways to deal with angry feelings:

- You can view the situation differently. While angry feelings frequently surprise you and come upon you automatically, it is your 'self-talk' that makes you angrier.

Change what you tell yourself about what is going on, and you can drastically change your feelings about it. In your example, try telling yourself things like a few minutes more won't matter," or "I'll speak to the officer about the issue when I have more time."

- Try to cool down – Relax and cool down. Once captured by intense angry feelings, you may become incapacitated and unable to solve problem or to obtain the information you need to deal with the issue. The solution is to cool down before doing anything.

You should look for alternatives. You can look for different ways to respond to the situation, before angry feelings overtake you. Maybe you can still get what you want without displaying angry behaviour. For instance, try to talk simply giving himinformation; "Are you aware that there is a long queue".

It is almost always better to try alternatives before expressing anger or aggression. In angry situation, you lose confidence.

52. Try To Improve Your Memory Power

Human memory depends upon various mental and physical factors. Your health plays an important role in your memory. Studies indicate that your memory depends mostly upon how you train your mind to remember and recall. Other factors include your level of interest, how important the memories are to you, and how frequently you may use them. It is easy to remember related and meaningful information than meaningless subjects and things.

Some people are good at remembering visual data and some are good at remembering verbal information. Birth related factors also play a role in memory. Some people are born with photographic memory, superhuman memory and selective memory. It is also possible to improve your memory and remember long lists of unrelated information with purely mechanical methods. Research has also been done to ascertain whether it is possible to boost memory through sleep, hypnosis and subliminal suggestions.

Good memory always develops confidence in you and your behaviour.

Ways to boost memory

Write down your important events. With the amount of things you have to remember in any given day, why should you try to stuff it all into your memory bank? When you want to remember something, the very best thing to do is write it down. Then, when you need to recall it, it will be there for you in an instant. Then it will automatically register in your memory.

Keep your notes together. When you write down things you want to remember, keep them in one consistent place. Otherwise, you're going to spend a lot of time looking for your notes.

- **For good health, you should eat healthy foods,** get enough sleep and exercise. These are all important for your memory, staying focused and being alert.

- **You can call yourself to remind things.** If you're at the office or outside house and you want to do something when you arrive home, call your answering machine and leave yourself a message. When you get home, you'll listen to your message and remember exactly what you wanted to do.

- **You should believe in yourself.** If you keep saying you have a bad memory, you'll probably continue to have a bad memory. It's important to have a motivated, I CAN remember attitude in your life.

- **Post-it notes can be helpful to boost memory.** Those wonderful, little sticky notes can be amazing memory helpers. Want to remember something before you leave the house? Jot it down on a Post-It Note and stick it on the inside of your door. You'll be sure to see it as you're getting ready to walk out. If you have to make an urgent call first thing in the morning? Post it will help. You can leave a Post-It Note on your telephone.

- **You can maintain e-mail reminders.** There are many free e-mail reminder services available. You simply type in what you want to remember, such as a birthday, anniversary or event and you then receive an e-mail reminder when the date is approaching. You can try http://www.calendar.yahoo.com

- **Visual reminders can help you** remember and focus. If your goal is to take a trip to a beautiful island in the next year, keep a magazine photograph of the island right on your desk. If your goal is to own your own business one day, find a picture or ornament that will help remind you of this goal each day. Visual reminders help you to make things easy and remember well.

- Timers and alarms are also helpful. Take advantage of alarm clocks of mobile and timers throughout the day. If you have to take the clothes for dry cleaning at 3:00? Set your alarm clock to remind you. Want to leave for the basketball game or gym by 6:15? Set your timer to beep a few minutes before.

53. Be good to yourself

- You might treat yourself badly as some people do so. You should realize that there is no need for doing that. Even if you have done up until today, you can choose to stop it. Be good to yourself instead. It's ok. It's allowed. It's pretty useless doing the opposite unless your goal is to make unhappy, complaining people happy.

- An important part of being good to yourself is recognizing your strengths and developing them. This will not only helps to improve your skills but also your confidence in your own abilities. Another smaller but important part is simply learning to accept a compliment. It's nice to say "thank you!" and feel good about yourself.

54. Improve your Social Skills

Relationships are one of the most important areas of life. I improving your social skills is one of the top things people want to learn. Improving your skills in this area and finding a larger confidence in your social skill can be a really big boost for your overall sense of confidence.

If you lack social skills, it's important to learn how to build social skills. There is a significant correlation between your social skills and your success in any area of life. With good social skills, it's easier to make friends, build strong relationships and get ahead in your career and gain a great confidence.

Ways to build social skills

If you lack social skills, it's important to learn how to build social skills. There is a significant correlation between your social skills and your success in any area of life. With good social skills, it's easier to make friends, build strong relationships and get ahead in your career and gain a great confidence.

1. Meeting with people

- You may be tempted to avoid social interactions because you think you lack social skills, but unfortunately, this only keeps you lacking social skills. The key to improving them is to interact with others no matter how capable you are right now.

- By meeting new people, conversing with them and getting to know them, you develop your intuition about people and you gradually become better at attuning to them and building a connection with them.

- Developing any ability is largely a matter of practice. In order to develop your social skills, you need to spend a lot of time interacting with new people.

2. Ask for Feedback

- You may ask people you know and you trust to give you feedback. To give you their perspective on how you come across socially, on your strengths and your weaknesses. They can do this casually while chatting, or fill in some sort of feedback form you can devise. This will give you time to improve yourself and gaining confidence.

- Although it's hard to adjust your interpersonal skills when you don't understand exactly how people see you and what effect certain sides of your personality have on them.

3. Work on Specific Goals

- There is quite a wide array of social skills and trying to develop them all at once cannot yield results. It will be impractical and you will be spreading yourself too thin.

- It will be a much better approach to pick one or two specific skills at a time and work on improving them. Only when you've made enough progress with them, you can advance to other interpersonal skills. Setting specific goals and working on them is the best way to get results.

- As your social skills build, you'll find yourself feeling more confident in social settings and connecting easier with others. These skills will open up a wide range of opportunities in your life. You can take advantage from those opportunities.

4. Interact with Socially Skilled People

- One of the best ways to gain social skills is to learn it from others. You interact with people who have good social skills, you study their mannerisms and you learn from them. You'll notice that just by doing this, your social skills will go up.

- When you'll study them intentionally and try on to learn from their conduct, these skills will go up even faster. Socially skilled individuals are an infinite source of wisdom and they are full of confidence.

You should keep a positive intake of information, influence and emotions. Much of the news and society brings a bleak and negative picture of both the world and yourself to your doorstep each day. Just like the people that surround you the information that surrounds you can affect you in big way. Don't just stay passive and take it all in. Choose what you want to watch, hear and read. Choose what's useful and beneficial for you.

55. Redefine Failure

You should redefine your failure. It is important that how you view failure controls how much your confidence drops before or after a failure. The definition of failure you are brought up with in society might not be the best and most useful to have. If you look at the most successful people you quickly notice that they have a different response to failure than the more common one. They don't take failure or rejection that seriously. They know it's not the end of the world if they fail. Instead they look at each failure and see the good part: What they can learn from it and improve next time.

You have to work on your skills to sharpen them. See failure or rejection not as something incredible negative that might end your life if it strikes. Redefine it in your mind to lessen the negative emotional impact and the fear. See failure simply as feedback on what you need to improve on. Listen to the advice the failure gives you and you will improve. And, by redefining failure this way your level of confidence will not take a drastic drop every time you fail or fear failure.

They have an abundance-mentality. They know that if their first business-venture fails it feels like crap for a while but it's ok in the long run. They learn from it and then they try again. If they are rejected for date, do they give up? Probably not. They know that next week or the week after they might find someone else that's interesting and ask them out.

They know that there are a lot of good people out there. That there are a lot of good business opportunities out there. But they have also learned that to become successful at anything you have to fail perhaps 5, 10, 20 times or more.

Meeting with people

Developing any ability is largely a matter of practice. In order to develop your social skills, you need to spend a lot of time interacting with new people.

By meeting new people, conversing with them and getting to know them, you develop your intuition about people and you gradually become better at attuning to them and building a connection with them.

- You may be tempted to avoid social interactions because you think you lack social skills, but unfortunately, this only keeps you lacking social skills. The key to improving them is to interact with others no matter how capable you are right now.

56. Be honest to yourself and others

Learning to be honest and eliminating the need for lies can help to clean up your conscience and your relationships. No one likes lies. But, unfortunately, being dishonest with others and ourselves is sometimes easier than telling the truth. It doesn't need to be that way. Shifting your perspective slightly and orienting yourself to a policy of honesty can help you to eliminate the need for lies and make it more attractive to tell the truth.

Do you ever wonder is it possible to be honest without being harsh? It's true that you should avoid telling the truth to keep away from hurting someone's feelings? If you do positive effort, it is possible to be comfortably honest with people in situations that require an offensive response. Candor is often the kindest and most honourable way to express you and yourself. You should avoid false flattery or mistaken confidence.

You should remember that honesty is the basis of all healthy relationships, whether with a friend, a significant relative, your spouse, co-worker or any other person. Honesty gives rise to trust, which is essential for maintaining relationships. Honesty also establishes consistency, allowing the other person to rely on what you say as carrying true meaning. This honesty makes you more confident. Most important of all, honesty is about respect and valuing the dignity of the other person.

Understand the things for being honest –

- Being honest is hard because it forces us to acknowledge our mistakes.

- If someone pressures you into telling the truth about something you did, then say such a thing as "I was wrong to make that thoughtless mistake; I will do better! Please give me another chance to show you I didn't mean it and that I can be a good friend".
- Written statements can reveal how many times you have been honest or dishonest. Learn from this knowledge. Recorded dishonesty can provide data for future decisions.
- For most people, keeping secrets to benefit someone is not considered dishonest if he or she will completely understand all matter upon finding out. The boundary between honest and dishonest secrecy is nevertheless fuzzy.

Remember the following things to learn to be honest-

1. To break the chain of embarrassment and lying, it's important to learn to anticipate things that you'll likely feel guilty about in the future, and avoid those behaviours. *For example,* if you smoke cigarettes, you won't have to lie if everyone knows it's true. Own up to it.

2. We've all lied at one time or another, to different people, to ourselves and for different reasons. Sometimes lies are made to look ourselves better. They might include exaggerations and embellishments.

Sometimes lies are told to cover up our bad behaviours, transgressions or any activity we're not proud of. *For example,* if your mom found a pack of cigarettes in your jacket, you might lie and say that they're your friend's to avoid punishment.

We lie to peers, we think, are better than us because we want them to respect us as we respect them. Unfortunately, being dishonest is disrespectful in the long run. You should give people more credit for their ability to empathize and understand you on a deeper level.

3. We lie to avoid embarrassment and punishment to ourselves. When we've done something we feel guilty about. Lies are told to eliminate the guilt, avoid the punishments and get back to the objectionable behaviour we're forced to lie about. It's a vicious cycle.

4. You must accept the consequence and decide to face them. Sometimes, it's better to own up to lies rather than continue weaving an elaborate web of lies. It can be liberating and extremely healthy to come clean.

5. Sometimes we lie to make ourselves seem bigger and better than we really are. Because we're constantly competing and comparing ourselves to others feeling competitive with others and give yourself the value you deserve, you won't feel the need to lie to bring yourself up.

6. You should avoid situations in which you'll have to lie for others. Be wary when someone tells you something in confidence *for example,* knowledge or involvement in a crime that you know that you should share with someone else. Hearing such information puts you in a difficult position. If someone begins a sentence with "Don't tell so-and-so about this, okay?" be prepared to say please don't tell me.

7. You should do things that make you feel pride. You don't have to lie if you feel good about yourself! Surround yourself with caring, understanding people who will respect you for who you are. Do things that give you pleasure and that make you feel proud of yourself.

8. You should always exercise tact. Learn to volunteer appropriate opinions. Everyone likes a straight-shooter. Consider the effect of your words and learn to rephrase possibly-offensive or uncomfortable language.

9. You can confront the things about yourself that you dislike. A big source of dishonesty in our lives comes from an unwillingness to confront the things about ourselves that we're ashamed of, embarrassed about, or just plain disgusted by. Without dwelling on them, you should try and define them honestly.

10. You should avoid unnecessary lies. Please don't add colour to your stories. It can be tempting, but you might be setting a precedent that opens up reasons and opportunities for more lies. Let the truth be the truth and be as honest as possible.

11. You can stay silent if you need to. If you're in a tense situation, in which getting honest would disrupt everyone's mood and happiness, it's not necessarily dishonest to remain silent. If you've got the option of staying out of it, stay out of it. It takes courage to stay silent in an awkward situation sometimes.

12. Forget what you think other people want to hear. Give other people the benefit of the doubt. Let your honesty impress people, not your exaggeration. Lots of dishonesty results from attempts to impress our peers with elaborate tales.

57. Walk faster with Confidence

Self-confidence is one's own view about himself and his capabilities. Walking is one of the most basic human tasks and usually won't require a conscious effort; therefore, walking takes the focus off his clothes and equipments and tells a lot about your personality. Understand the following things –

1. Walking depicts a person's ability to carry oneself in any kind of situation.

2. Walking faster can improve one's self-confidence in a variety of ways. It has been found by surveys that people who walk faster are seen as important people. Walking a bit faster would make an impression that you are busy and are involved in significant tasks. It is all about making a self-image for others to see.

3. When walking faster to communicate a message of self-confidence, one must not overdo it to the extent of looking exasperated. It's just a matter of carrying a comfortable self.

4. When walking, one should not stare at the road or at the floor you must hold your head up and maintain it at eye level. This will create opportunities to make eye contact with other people. It's a non-verbal method to say "hi, how are you?"

5. Walking doesn't require much effort however; walking with confidence requires practice and devotion. Walking can deliver numerous benefits in different levels to the person especially in terms of self-confidence. Walking tall is being tall amidst all the challenges in one's life. So, you can see how can one's self-confidence be portrayed in walking?

58. Dress sharp to Gain Confidence

The way you dress is a huge part of the image of yourself you put out in to the world. It's a massive part of people's first impressions and it affects the way they treat you. Instead of lamenting the superficiality of the modern condition – work with it! Dressing sharply (whatever your profession) demonstrates a level of competence, confidence and present ability. Looking like the man you want to be not only allows you to see potential in yourself, but will help others do the same.

An important aspect of being a sharp dressed man is that it can help you develop long-term goals for personal achievement.

Have you ever noticed how you always stand up straighter with your shirt tucked in? Or how you hold yourself differently in a suit than a pair of jeans? Clothing effects the way you move and behave not only because it physically constricts you, but because it makes you feel a certain way.

Dressing the style changes everything. It may not be everything. Still becoming a well dressed person will change how society perceives you.

Clothes affect how we feel when we leave the house. The last glance in the mirror before we face the rest of the world can make or break your confidence.

It is a fact that no one is more critical of your appearance than yourself. Dressing to impress does not have to be expensive, it just requires your attention to think about what will make you feel good and confident when leaving the house providing that it is clean and ironed.

It is actually not surprising that most people have no idea how to dress. Most guys will copy what their friends are wearing, happy to fit in and not attract any unnecessary attention. Some go one step further, emulating looks on billboards or in lifestyle magazines. Others try to show off with luxury brands.

It's not difficult to dress well. It certainly requires far less money than most assume. However, it requires some patience and a willingness to try something new. The first step involves a change of mindset.

Some typical consequences of looking sharp are following:

- You will feel more confident and at ease.
- You will hear smart comments from people who can't dress well.
- You will get more attention and compliments, especially from opposite sex.
- You will develop an appreciation for others who make an effort to look good.

Do the following things to dress sharp and to develop confidence-

1. You have to convince yourself that it's good to dress well. This is very important. Become comfortable with the idea of permanently changing how you look.

2. You should realize that there is a big difference between fashion and style. Fashion is about showing off the latest in designer trends, while men's style rarely changes over time.

The goal of dressing sharp is not to have the clothing to do the talking for you. Instead, the idea is to find and develop your own image by dressing sharp. It is a way of showing the world who you are, even before you do or say anything.

3. You must also understand that this is a lifelong project. One does not become stylish overnight. It will take time to work out the details.

4. It is general rule that the more fit you are, the better most clothing will look on you. So try to make your physique perfect so that you look smarter.

5. To dress well, you must avoid wearing tacky or distracting clothing. The best way to protect yourself from committing major style crimes is to give all unnecessary clothing away *for example:*

- Try to avoid anything with visible branding or logos.
- Avoid torn or patterned jeans. It is completely unnecessary. Keep it simple, stick to dark preferably unwashed denim.

6. Remember that everything you wear must fit well. This is non-negotiable. Shirts should not puff out at the waist. Suits should fit like a glove, but alterations will be necessary for any suit bought off the rack.

Pants and jeans should not be baggy, or skin tight either. You should aim for a "slim straight" fit.

7. You can start introducing your own ideas and modifications and start seeking out individual items that you know would work great in your wardrobe. Chances are, you are already somewhat of a style icon in your local community or social circles.

8. Being appropriately well-dressed helps you feel confident and at ease with your surroundings rather than worried about being under-dressed or out of place. If you iron and starch your shirt, you will feel the difference it makes to the way you move. Your movements will be more careful and refined because of the small effort you've put in. A feeling of confidence will be in your head.

Leaving a good impression through walking is a whole different thing from getting the actual benefits of walking.

People walk all the time. People would tend to look at the street rather than put their heads up and look at the people who are walking along with them. Some would stare at big billboards and advertisements or take out their phones from their pockets and pretend to call someone and do other stuff while walking. These are common signs of poor self-confidence. These are all manifested in walking.

59. Look Good Feel Good

As most people know well, looking fine can be easy, but looking sharp is hard. There is something about a well-dressed man, whether in a uniform or a blazer that suggests strength of character and body. The thoughtfulness and attention are required to look sharp. The strength and carefulness are required to stay. These are not signs of fussy self-consciousness but demonstrate strength and a keen self-awareness.

Try to remember following things to look good and feel good:-

1. **If you get noticed, you stand out.**

It can be hard to get noticed sometimes. With more and more competition in the workforce, coupled with easier access to low-cost, it becomes difficult to stand out. The sharp-dressed person gets noticed amongst the crowd because he is different.

2. **You should know that great style takes time.**

Great style is not about trying to keep up with the latest trends of the moment, it is about finding a personal style that is comfortable and that works for you. There is nothing stylish or attractive about a person who is totally inappropriately dressed for the life he lives. But no matter who you are: Whatever your job, income, or tastes, it is completely possible to live with style. Trends and fashions come and go, and will no doubt influence your style.

3. Style is highly personal and takes a lifetime. Being a sharp dressed man and looking good is about care, thoughtfulness, and respect for yourself and others. If you can dress in a way that combines elements of your own personality and style, as well as the person you strive to be, it will be a good day indeed.

4. Use your wardrobe to work towards being the person you want to be.

5. Think of being well-dressed as an act of self- discipline. Caring about the way you look is not only important, but also a subtle display of strength.

6. Stand out from the crowd. Make your style personal and rise above the rest.

7. Think style not fashion. Style is a personal thing that takes a lifetime to develop and refine. Getting dressed is about being yourself and looking like who you want to be.

8. If you look good, you will and vice versa if you feel good, you will look good feel good. You should use clothing to set the tone for your performance, feelings and attitude throughout the day.

60. Trust in your abilities and power

The important is that **"nobody can make you feel inferior without your consent".** You just have to believe that for ourselves.

By projecting a confident perception of yourself to others, you can make the perception a reality and give your confidence a boost. It is not easy to stay confident, especially when confronted with a situation beyond your control, but there are a number of ways you can take control of your life and the best way to start is by consciously building your self-confidence first.

What is the first image you want others to see? Is it your slumped shoulders, arms folded to hide your stomach, eyes looking down? Or is it your great posture, head held high and attentive eyes? Shake off that poor posture and stand tall. Your body and your confidence will thank you for it. You will instantly feel more awake, in control and confident by raising your eye level to those around you and opening yourself to engagement with others. Making eye contact is nerve-racking at the beginning, but stay firm and it will become second nature in no time.

Do you feel confident regardless of the situations you are in?

Self-confidence means assuredness in your own worth, abilities and power, regardless of the situation you are in. Someone who is self-confident has a strong sense of belief and certainty in himself / herself. The person, who persons calmness, composure and is self-aware.

Self-confidence is often linked with possessing of certain knowledge, skill sets or abilities, whether it is acquired or innate. While having aptitude in a particular area can help booster your self-worth. Someone with absolutely no competency in something can still be self-confident.

Understand Behaviour of Low-Confident Persons

Have you ever known someone who has low self-confidence? Have you noticed how does this person come across to you? A person who has a lack of self-confidence has a lack of self belief, usually caused by a sense of uncertainty about one thing or another.

People with low self-confidence tend to make distance with people around them. Their limiting mindsets and behaviors make them feel 'heavy'. These people vibrate in consciousness levels of Pride. They usually face levels of shame, guilt, apathy and fear.

Lack of self-confidence is a crippling trait because it often limits you in your opportunities and jeopardizes your chances of success, which leads to a self-fulfilling prophecy.

Here, are some typical behaviors of people with low self-confidence:

1. Being overly shy and reserved
2. Overly critical of themselves
3. Undervaluing what they are capable of
4. Doing things to please others
5. Taking blame even when it is not their fault
6. Having a fearful and adverse attitude toward most things

7. Being hung up over negative outcomes and 'failures' in the past.

If you lack self-confidence, you will predict you will not be able to deliver to expectations. What do you think will happen next? This lack of self-belief is going to influence the thoughts and actions that you undertake. When you are constantly thinking about a negative outcome, it takes your focus off what you should be doing to achieve a desirable outcome. Because an undesirable outcome is manifested, your belief gets enforced and you continue to have low self-confidence.

Thus, having self-confidence is an asset to you in life. It not only puts you at a better and more positive emotional and mental state, it also sets you up toward getting what you want. It equips you to conquer your challenges. Having self-confidence enables you to fearlessly pursue your biggest dreams.

61. Don't decide your worth on the basis of social perceptions

The presumptions of what represents worth are largely due to social perceptions. All the beliefs that we need to have certain skills, certain behaviors, etc. to be confident have all been conditioned in the society, rather than being hard truths.

Think about a symbol of worth to you. Is it competency? Is it the amount of money you earn? Is it how attractive you look? Identify them first. Then, ask yourself this – why do you perceive these as symbols of worth? Why must you have to have these before you can feel worthy or confident about yourself? Who said anything about these being prerequisites before you can even feel your self-worth?

The problem that needs to be addressed is the attachment to these symbols with one's worth. All your beliefs on what represents worth can only be true if you allow them to be true. The key is to break the linkage between all perceptions and your own assessment of worth. If you don't see money as a valuation of your worth, then it won't. If you don't see attractiveness as what makes you worthy, then it won't. Remember, these are merely external objects, and not you.

It is wisely said – "Confidence is not a guarantee of success, but a pattern of thinking that will improve your likelihood of success, a tenacious search for ways to make things work."

Whenever you see any circumstance where you do not feel self-confident – ask yourself: Why am I not feeling self-confident? Where is this uncertainty coming from? What am I attaching my self-worth to?

When you become aware of what you are linking your worth to, start releasing yourself of that limiting belief that you can only feel worthy or confident in the face of certain prerequisites. If you do that, you will find yourself filled with a sense of self-worth. You will find this self-worth will be what leads you to outcomes you desire. Afterwards you will feel more confident.

62. Make decision to be Confident

If you just make the decision to be confident, you don't need a reason. You don't need people to tell you that you're amazing, or you're beautiful, or we love you. You just have to like – "You know what? Today, I'm going to give myself a little bit of credit of this success. Today, I'm feeling more confident.

That's it. That's the power of intention. It's the power of the self-directed human being that you just get to choose how you want to feel.

You could be happy right now for no reason. You could tell others, "You know what, I've decided to be happy in my life." You don't need many things to make you happy.

People overcomplicate these things. They think that they need some big long psychological story one day to be more confident. No they don't need so.

So, you should set the intention to be a confident human being? Why not set the intention to be a loving person or an ambitious person or a fun loving person or a flirty person or a sexy person, or whatever kind of person that you want to be? Just decide - you don't need a bunch of stuff from others.

You should feel like-

"I'm going to be confident. I'm just going to allow that to come up. I'm going to feel that sense and feeling what confidence is for me and express that genuinely and real for myself."

If your brain stem comes up with worry, concern, fear, the paying attention to what is wrong you can fix it, flee or escape. You have to have intention for who you are and what you're going to be. It begins with you simply deciding to be a confident person.

You should get over your own qualities and one day just realizes that real confidence is simply having the ability to genuinely express who you truly are and to pursue things that you truly desire. That's confidence.

63. Have the sense of Integrity

Every human being develops in its psyche. We develop a real sense of confidence coming from a sense of integrity for ourselves. Integrity is, "I know who I am and I'm being that, consistently. I know what I want and I am chasing that consistently."

Being aligned with who you are, your values, your beliefs and your dreams, having integrity, that gives us confidence in self. In that way our self can stand on its own and be itself and do what it desires. That gives us a sense of confidence.

Have you been really demonstrating who you are to the world? Have you allowed yourself to do that? If you do that over a period of time, you gain a sense of confidence.

Confidence comes from that and that too is will, it is decision, it is a desire to want to be a person of integrity and confidence, and that's where it stems from.

There's a cohesive sense of identity that comes from being consistent to the best of who we are.

As you develop skills and abilities in your life in your unique areas, you become more confident.

64. Momentum is Key to Confidence

Often, some of the best decisions in your life come after you have momentum at something and then you've gained some more perspective. But a lot of people are waiting for the perfect plan, the perfect time, the perfect person, the perfect thing to pursue our goals or our dreams and it's that waiting that often dampens their confidence.

When we stop having any momentum in our life we often feel lost, confused or down. We start losing that connection with our strength and our self. So we have to take more action to develop more confidence. That means we have to say, "What is it I truly want," and then start moving towards it.

A lot of people think that their decision is their destiny. A lot of people decide to do something good, but they don't.

As soon as you take the first step to do something, a feeling comes in your mind, "Hey, I took a step. That is good for me" and then you start making better and better decisions, because you are able to do and see more.

Often you don't know where you are going in life until you start jogging towards something. Something you run just in place, sometimes run somewhere, but as soon as you actually run, things open up to you and you say oh, look at this.

People often say, "I wish I had more vision for my life." It's hard to have vision for your life if you've never seen anything. Get outside of the house, turn off the TV, turn off your computer, go and see the world a little bit, you'll gain a little bit more vision and momentum towards the things you want, you will have more confidence.

You have to realize your strength there is no reason in the world that you cannot, yourself, with very simple moves, gain more momentum. More momentum means more progress and more progress means more confidence.

65. Suround Yourself with Supportive People

We all need people around us who are supportive, positive and buoyant and who appreciate our sense of aliveness, joy and happiness in life.

And, if you don't have that, go get around people who are positive and who are amazing.

A lot of people will tell you, "Hey what should I do? I can't get rid of all those negative people of myself." Sometimes negative people in your life are your mom or your dad, your lover, your spouse, or one of your kids. For your loved ones your friends You can't just open the door and say, "Get out of here". It doesn't work like that. It will be really bad to do so.

It's not about cutting loose all the negative people, of chopping off people and getting rid of them. What you have to do is to say to yourself instead, "If I don't have the supportive peer group, let me go and create that. Let me find those people and get around them."

When people will be cheering you, you gain more confidence. You allow yourself to feel that sense of success and sense of integrity, when other people recognize it in you.

Sometimes our greatest confidence comes from having a community of supporters. So you don't have to wait for those supporters to show up, you should try to find them. Go and mingle. Get outside of the house, live life again. What do you notice? You notice more integrity, more momentum, more competency, more good people. Suddenly that thing you were hoping one day you find, *i.e.,* you find confidence. One day when you wake up, you find you created it yourself.

66. Become a Positive Thinker

Having a positive outlook is a choice and that makes you confident. You can choose to think thoughts that elevate your mood, throw a more constructive light on difficult situations, and generally colour your day with brighter, more hopeful approaches to the things you do. By choosing to take a positive outlook on life, you can begin to see life as filled with possibilities and solutions instead of worries and obstacles

Choosing to think more positively will not only help you to take control of your life and make your everyday experiences more pleasant, but it will have countless benefits to on your mental and physical health. Being aware of these benefits can help you be more motivated to think positively on a regular basis.

Here are some of the most important benefits of positive thinking:

- Better mental and physical well-being
- A more natural ability to form relationships and create bonds
- An increased life span
- Better coping skills during times of stress
- Greater resistance to the common cold and fever
- Lower rates of depression and distress.

You should remember that you experience about

thousands of thoughts every day in your life. And they're your own thoughts. Nobody controls how you feel and think unless you let them. This might seem like a very challenging idea if you're absorbing the emotions and preferences of other people, but you're always making a choice to think positively or negatively. Always try to be a positive thinker; this will certainly increase your confidence.

Positive thinkers have better stress coping skills, stronger immunity and a lower risk of cardiovascular disease. Taking an optimistic view rather than negative thoughts can benefit your overall mental well-being.

67. Stop Negative Thinking

You should make a decision to stop being a negative thinker. That means deciding to conquer the negativity that is going on around you and there will always be plenty of it. Think of what you can do today that is good for you and others that is positive and constructive. Decide how you will react in ways that will make a difference to your life.

How to stop negative thinking-

Your plan can be simple. you can vow to identify and record your negative thoughts each day. Then you take time to reflect on why you had those thoughts and how you can improve them.

- Don't let other people ruin your plan and thinking. People will often make things seem more important or worrisome than they really are. By not allowing yourself to be swept away by that enhanced anxiety. Instead taking time to think it over and get an answer that works, you'll feel less pressured.
- As you continue to execute your plan, you'll see that identifying your negative thoughts becomes easier and maintaining a negative attitude will be harder.
- If you make a plan to be more positive, it will be a move in the right direction. This will help you to stay positive because you will feel a greater sense of control over your life and your choices.
- In order to shift away from the negative thinking that is

holding you back from having a positive outlook, you'll need to become more aware of your "automatic negative thoughts". When you recognize them, you're in a position to challenge them and give them their marching orders to move out of your mind.

- Once you identify the negative thought, battle this kind of thinking and counteract this thought with positive thoughts in the opposite direction.

- You should try music, read books on positive thinking and stop seeing violating movies. Music benefits your mind really well and books would give always good tricks to stop negative thinking while violating movies affect our mind negatively.

You can go to a peaceful place where there are beautiful landscapes and pleasant comfortable weather. It lays really a good impact on mind and improves negative thinking.

You should Avoid Negative Self-Talk.

Self-talk means the things you mentally tell yourself. You think of this as the inner voice inside your mind that analyzes how you perform and interact in the world around you. Remember if your self-talk concentrates on negative thoughts, your self-esteem will suffer. If you start thinking critical thoughts about yourself, you should take a moment to pause and assess.

You should know how to turn negative self-talk into positive self-talk. You can start by noticing their thought patterns and then focus on changing these into more positive ones. When you catch yourself engaging in a negative thought, mentally telling yourself to "Stop" can help break the pattern.

68. Avoid personalizing the faults

You should avoid "personalizing faults". Personalizing is thinking that anything that goes wrong is automatically your fault. It is liable to make you feel terrible in almost any situation. If you take this type of thinking too far, you can think that no one likes you or wants to talk with you and that way every little move you make is going to disappoint someone.

Sometime you absorb the feelings of others and feel guilty. This is the way someone who is used to absorbing people's feelings thinks. Here is an example. You may think, "My girl friend didn't smile at me this morning. I must have done something to upset her." However, it's most likely that your girl friend was just having a bad mood; you'll only get frustrated if you think of what you could have done to hurt her.

You should be rational. You should slow down and think of all the other reasons a negative situation might happen.

69. Avoid assuming and filter thinking

Do you know, what is filter thinking? I tell you. When you choose to only hear the negative message in something communicated to you, this is filter thinking. For example, your elder brother boss might have praised you on a job well done, but mentioned a small area where you might make a few changes next time. Your brother is trying to help you identify where you could improve a few minor issues. But in your mind you're too busy turning this feedback into a damning criticism, failing to see the gigantic praise that came your way. If you think like this, then you'll never see the positive things in any situation.

If you want to avoid filter thinking, you should reflect on the entire situation and even take notes. Make a list of all of the things that were said, positive and negative. If you write down everything your brother said to you during a positive meeting, then you'll have visual confirmation that the positive comments greatly outweigh the negative ones.

Assuming things in negative way is called catastrophizing. This is when you can't think of anything without assuming it's all going to end in doom and gloom. It's unrealistic, and it is very exhausting to keep thinking this way. *For example,* you might think that your entire family will be hit by a bus during that day, all because you didn't bid them goodbye. Here's how you can avoid catastrophe thinking:

- To minimize catastrophic thinking, you should avoid television programmes that promote the idea that gruesome murder or tragic accidents are an everyday occurrence.

- You should be practical to avoid such assuming and catastrophizing.

70. Live an Optimistic Life to develop Confidence

Developing a positive attitude is actually the development of a skill. You're not born thinking negatively – it happens over time as you absorb the world around you, including how you were raised, educated, and treated through life. As with any skill, it takes time to master and it requires dedicated practice and gentle reminders about not falling back into negative thinking. Thus, you will be able to live an optimistic life.

If you say positive things about yourself, regularly, this affects your thinking and your emotions, as well as your self-esteem.

Be sure to praise yourself for things done well. You deserve to acknowledge the good you've achieved and the efforts you made. Treat yourself to something good and keep it as a memento of that achievement. This will bring hope and optimism in your life.

Spend time with optimistic people, Optimism is infectious. If you want to be infected by optimism, you should associate with optimistic people, who can provide something of value you should spend time with such people. You should look for the positives in other people too – finding what is good in people and accentuating that will help more of it to flourish. You should learn to compliment people around you.

You should avoid making friends with a negative outlook, unless you really care about that person and want to change their thoughts.

You should avoid people who sap your energy and motivation. If you can't avoid them, or don't want to, learn how not to let them get you down. You can keep your connection with them very brief and short.

71. Try to do new things

Experiencing a wide variety of life can do wonders in your life. If you Step out of your comfort zone, it can often take you by surprise and knock out those negative feelings you have. Something as simple as trying a new food in a restaurant can lead to the discovery of new tastes and different sensations, along with the release of negative prior impressions. Here, are some other new things that can help put a positive spin on your life and have confidence-

- Learn a new skill, such as singing or any other skill of your choice
- Visit a new town, city, or country and see how other people view the world
- Take up learning an instrument, or Sudoku, or learn a new language
- Read a novel you've never considered before
- Take an acting class. This is a great way to express yourself and move out of your comfort zone
- Write your thoughts and imagination. That can create your stories.

72. Be more aware of your surrounding

By forcing yourself to notice people, listen attentively, feel the things happening to you with grace and care and to remain aware of what is happening, you'll find that it's much more enjoyable to be positive and gaining knowledge. Thus, you will develop confidence in yourself. Negative thinking is often an excuse to live in a fixed routine procedure, stay on autopilot and to stop really seeing and experiencing the world and other beings. It's a form of creating a shield around oneself and shutting down on being present and is mentally lazy.

To know how being more aware can make your life more positive, you can do the following things-

1. Try taking a yoga class. Yoga can also help you become more aware of the world as you get in touch with your breathing.

2. Consider taking up meditation as a way to centre yourself and learn excellent focus. By meditating every day for 10 to 20 minutes, you can increase your awareness of self and the present, helping you to correct the stinking thinking with greater consciousness. That will surely give you confidence.

3. If you know what is happening around you in the world, you'll be better able to recognize your own behaviour and be gentle with yourself rather than beating yourself up for mistakes. You'll learn to understand your body.

73. Try Humour to lessen stress

It can be really difficult to stay calm under stress, But you can do so, if there is little humour or lightness in your life. Even when you are facing challenges, it is important to stay open to laughter and humor. Sometimes, simply recognizing the potential humour in a situation can lessen your stress.

Learn to have fun and humour. It can even brighten your outlook. Seeking out sources of humour such as watching funny video or reading jokes online can help you think more positive thoughts. Now-a-days has lot of funny videos and jokes to entertain you and to present humour in your life.

For example, if you have low self confidence in your job, it may be because you are lacking the information and know ledge of how to perform well.

Competency in anything can always be developed via preparation, practice and experience. The key to developing competency is to engage in knowledge acquisition and repeatedly do it to the point you can. *For example,* if it's an academic subject, read up as much as you can through different sources, if it's a sport or technique, keep training every day, if it's giving a presentation or public speaking, continuously practice in front of different audiences to build up the skill sets. In the same way if it's something social like talking to a stranger, just start with small goals of talking to one stranger every day. Eventually, you will find yourself so competent in the area that you become naturally self-confident in it.

Some people seek knowledge and competency to gain status symbols and titles. Some people strive for successes in everything they do. The problem with acquiring symbols of worth to increase self-confidence is the boost in self-confidence. But it only lasts as long as the symbols are valid. If they were to be removed from you or lose their relevance, your self-confidence will change accordingly.

Imagine a tennis badminton who measures his worth based on his victories in his badminton games. He keeps practicing to increase his odds of victories. Whenever he wins, his self-confidence gets a boost; however whenever he loses, his self-confidence gets a hit.

If you really want to gain knowledge, you have to get close attachment with learned people. You have to ask questions and learn from them. You must be enthusiastic to do this. Read as many books as you can. Connect to the internet for best webs that can give you good knowledge. Meet experienced people and talk to them that are the best way to gain knowledge.

74. Control Your Temper

Keeping your temper in check can be challenging

Do you fume when someone cuts you off in traffic? Does your blood pressure rocket when your child refuses to cooperate? Anger is a normal and even healthy emotion – but it's important to deal with it in a positive way. Uncontrolled temper can take a toll on both your health and your relationships.

You should be ready to get your temper and anger under control. You can start by considering these anger management tips.

1. Once you're calm, express your anger

First of all, try to be calm after losing temper. As soon as you're thinking calmly and clearly, express your frustration in an assertive but express in a non- confrontational way. State your concerns and needs clearly and directly, without hurting others or trying to control them.

2. Think before you speak

In the heat of the moment, it's easy to say something wrong, you'll later regret. Take a few moments to collect your thoughts before saying anything in anger.

3. Take a timeout

Give yourself short breaks during times of the day that tend to be stressful. A few moments of quiet time might help you feel better prepared to handle what is ahead without getting irritated or angry.

4. Get some exercise

Physical activity can help reduce stress that can cause you to become angry. If you feel your anger escalating, go for a brisk walk or run, or spend some time doing other enjoyable physical activities. It will reduce anger.

5. Use humor to release tension

Lightening up can help diffuse tension. Use humor to help you face what's making you angry and, possibly, any unrealistic expectations you have for how things should go. Avoid sarcasm, though – it can hurt feelings and make things worse.

6. Know when to seek help

Learning to control anger is a challenge for everyone at times. Consider seeking help for anger issues if your anger seems out of control–, causes you to do things you regret or hurts those around you.

7. Practice relaxation skills

When your temper flares, put relaxation skills to work. Practice deep-breathing exercises, imagine a relaxing scene, or repeat a calming word or phrase, such as, "Take it easy." You might also listen to music, write in a journal or do a few yoga poses – whatever it takes to encourage relaxation.

8. Don't hold a grudge

Forgiveness is a powerful tool. If you allow anger and other negative feelings to crowd out positive feelings, you might find yourself swallowed up by your own bitterness or sense of injustice. But if you can forgive someone who angered you, you might both learn from the situation. It's unrealistic to expect everyone to behave exactly as you want at all times.

9. Stick with 'I' statements

To avoid criticizing or placing blame – which might only increase tension – use "I" statements to describe the problem. Be respectful and specific. *For example,* say, "I'm upset that you left the table without offering to help with the dishes," instead of, "You never do any housework."

10. Identify possible solutions

Instead of focusing on what made you anger and lose temper, work on resolving the issue at hand. Does your child's messy room or null biting habit drive you crazy? Is your partner late for dinner every night or he/she being in watching TV, remind yourself that anger won't fix anything and might only make it worse?

75. Recognize Your Insecurities

1. One of the biggest issues is insecurity. More people exhibit forms of insecurity than you would guess. Recognizing the insecurity can help you communicate better with the person.

2. Interpersonal relationships are difficult at times because we do not recognize the underlying issues driving the other person.

3. First, determine your own insecurities. Dealing with them will make you more able to determine insecurities in others.

How to Recognize?

This is a lesson in learning about yourself and your insecurities but will also help later on in dealing with others.

Ask yourself a few questions and answer them on paper.

Questions to ask yourself include:

- Do I believe I am always correct and argue for my point of view a lot? Do I shy away from contributing comments in meetings?
- Do I believe everyone else is smarter than I am?
- Do I constantly look for approval from more than one person?

- Do I believe everyone else is dumber than I am?
- Do I demand my own way at home to the exclusion of everyone else, including my spouse?
- Do I have to flaunt my intelligence?
- Do I constantly interrupt because I think my comments are more important than the other person's?
- Do I drink or do drugs when life gets too difficult?
- Do I fall apart when I am criticized?
- Am I very critical of everyone?
- Do I use violence at home to make my point?

After answering these questions, ask yourself what changes you can make on your own. A lot of them simply require stopping that behavior. Stopping yourself from being overcritical may not rid you of your underlying insecurity at first. Once you begin to look for the ways to praise another person, you will realize there is more good than bad in both others and yourself. Sometimes working on changing the behavior can work faster to get good results, both in our outward behavior to others and in understanding what brought us to behave this way in the first place. Putting blame on someone else for the way we behave does not change our behavior; it only gives us permission to excuse ourselves.

Ultimately, it does not matter how we were raised or what tragedies occurred in our lifetime. We are responsible for our behavior and the choices we make. You should take responsibility for your insecurities and work to change your behavior. If you fear contributing at meetings and you know the subject matter, contribute an idea or a comment. Start with one, but don't allow yourself to shrink away if the first idea is not accepted by others. Keep trying.

Talking about your own intelligence or how high your IQ is does not earn you their respect. It makes you boring and viewed as either a braggart or a snob. You should avoid conversations that lead you to discuss your intelligence. Put your fingers crossed every time you interrupt. Soon you will think before your speak. Allow the other person to finish his/her comments. Try to listen to what the person is thinking instead of trying to think about your next sentence.

You should realize that other people also have some of the same insecurities. Your attitude should be compassionate. Don't feel superior because you are working on high post. If someone interrupts you and others, you can take him aside and kindly bring it to his attention.

For people who shrink or sit quietly in meetings and those who may indicate to you they don't think of themselves as very smart, you can remind them of what they have accomplished. You should complement the people when they do a great job. We all need positive recognition.

76. Keep Your Body Language Fit and Fine

Body language is a big part of animal communication and humans have it too. They reveal through many gestures, postures and action thoughts that are not revealed in speech.

Speech is the primary mode of communication among humans. Humans evolved language as a powerful tool and have been using it effectively for long.

However, body language is more natural and subconscious. People may not even be aware that they are giving off signs that reveal their true thoughts. Learning to notice these is the key to being a good communicator.

The author after several years of research, the book provides a lot of insights into the subtle signals that the body gives off while talking. He explains how. You know legs might reveal what a person actually wants to do. How handshakes can be used to assert power and control. A smile can create a good impression.

There are some common gestures of liars and the common gestures that each person uses during courtship. Different gestures are used by people in different age groups in the same situation. Gestures and postures get more subtle as the person grows older and learns to control his body language.

You should how to use body signals and cues to communicate more effectively, how to control them to manipulate other people. You can learn comprehensive guide on the secret language of the body that mostly speaks the truth even while the mouth is uttering lies.

77. Bounce Back From your Mistakes

We all make mistakes. Over the course of your professional life, you can count on making a few bad career choices. Many of those mistakes can really drag you down. Recovering from them is definitely not a trivial matter.

Tips-

Here, are a few tips on how to effectively bounce back to grow stronger, when you make a bad result or make a mistake:

1. **Own your mistake.**

   One important thing is that you should own it when you commit a mistake. It is possible that circumstances were against you, or somebody, you counted on, failed you, or you just had a bad day. But great people don't blame others when things go wrong.

2. **Apologize to anyone affected.**

   You should realize your mistake and apologize to the concerned person. Make it a real apology, like "I'm sorry I caused all that downtime", not something lame and self-protective, like "I wish it hadn't happened".

3. **Find the root cause**

   If you systematically analyze your mistakes, you will realize there are patterns in your performance that contribute to these errors. Once you realize that, you are well on the way to fixing that rood cause.

4. Don't pretend accept it: Try to fix it if you can, and tell the concerned person.

Don't try to be a "quiet fixer." Mistakes often have side effects, and pretending that it didn't happen is dangerous. Hidden problems become serious threats eventually. If problems are revealed for everyone to see, it will get solved. Because once problems have been visualized, even if people didn't notice them earlier, they will rack their brains to find solutions to them.

5. Share what you learned.

In some environments, problem and solution sharing can be a lifesaver. It can help others to learn with your experience.

6. Reflect on the mistake.

You should think about mistake what caused it, and what you did that contributed to the situation. You can't learn anything from external factors, so think about them yourself.

Adopting these practices it may not make mistakes any less embarrassing, but it will help prevent disasters and ensure that you do not make the same mistake twice.

78. Identify your Success with your Skills & Accomplishments

The better you can describe your skills and accomplishments, the stronger the impression you'll make on your employers, friends and known persons. If you make a good impression, you gain self-confidence.

How to identify your accomplishments

Your accomplishments are what you achieve when you use your skills. They're the highlights of your best experiences. To find a new job to new employers, you need to identify and describe your accomplishments.

Work-related accomplishments can sometimes be hard to recognize, especially when they seem like just part of your job.

You can ask yourself to be sure to know about your accomplishment.

- What am I most proud of?
- What do I do better than my co-workers?
- What would my former employer(s) miss most about me?

You should use your accomplishment to get a good job and you will automatically gain confidence.

79. Identify Your Uniqueness to Attract Success and Confidence

To get ahead and win in your life, you need to know what is unique about you. As individuals we are all unique and when you are able to identify your uniqueness, instead of struggling, you'll attract the success you want. It's a simple enough step but not necessarily easy to accomplish. One reason for this is that the things that are unique about you, you generally take them for granted and are a natural part of who you are and you do.

There needs to be consistent inspired actions to integrate your ideal profile into all that you are and you do. But most people don't get this the way you must know this.

Identifying your uniqueness is an ongoing process and will impact your vision, mission and purpose. The process may also reveal some new products or services you want to offer. If you work for an organisation, it will be a heart-centred way of standing out from the crowd and letting you uniqueness shine forth. If you are focusing on it, it will help you to identify the work you're most drawn to doing and the people you most want to work with.

Identifying, what's unique about you, can be done initially by spending some time exploring this in writing and by having conversations with people you trust. Some of the best insights into your uniqueness will come if you are open to seeing them. You should have the idea of identifying your uniqueness and realising that these opportunities may come when you least expect them.

You should start to write down what you see as unique about you. Do you know this will include things that are a natural part of which you are and things you take for granted which others perhaps don't easily realise? You should choose to be with the process of identifying your uniqueness so that you can be aware of any new insights. These new insights may be the most powerful you have ever had.

80. Building Self-Confidence with the Mirror Technique

"Smile in the mirror. Do that every morning and you'll start to see a big difference in your life, it is an intelligent saying.

One of the most important characteristics of great people is self-confidence. Every successful person looks strong and confident and you will hardly believe that one time he used to be just an ordinary person with fears and worries. Even if you pretend that you are self-confident, you will look stronger in the eyes of the others and people will treat you with the respect you deserve.

These successful persons are not afraid to look someone in the eyes, to say what they want and to go and get it. They radiate confidence, power, success and determination. Many times this helps them win a fight and get what they want without even saying anything.

Can you imagine, they had gone through many difficulties until they've become what they are. The important thing is that everyone can achieve it.

Being self-confident means you believe in yourself. You have your goals set and work on them every day. Then you are not afraid to make eye contact. You feel you are unstoppable once you've decided something. It also helps you to speak and walk more confidently, look better and feel comfortable with yourself.

One simple exercise can separate you from all that. This is a technique that most of the people you look up to use every day. This is the mirror technique. Many businessmen, athletes, actors, motivational speakers, professors and many other successful persons do this. They do it every morning/evening, before a competition/meeting/performance/etc., or every time they need a little confidence boost and it has helped them more than anything.

What is the Mirror Technique

Stand in front of a big mirror. Straighten your back and take a deep breath with your chest. Look yourself in the eyes confidently. Put a light smile on your face so that you look determined. Start talking to your reflection. Say things like "I believe in myself!", "I can!", "I know what I want" and "I am not afraid to get it." "Every day I will get 1% better."

Think about the things you want to achieve and say that you can get them and there is nothing that can stop you on your way to success. Continue breathing as deep as you can and generate only positive statements and thoughts.

Go on like that for at least 5-10 minutes. You can always make it longer and add things like what you love most about you, your best qualities and recognitions. It is about starting to believe in yourself, your potential and possibilities.

Actually our subconscious is very susceptible to the things you say out loud. Imagine how big influence this technique will have on it when you combine saying positive statements while looking yourself confidently in the eyes. The best thing to understand that is to perform the exercise.

When to do?

It is best to do it in the morning. This way you can start your day with energy and go out with confidence. Otherwise you can prefer doing it in the evening or any other convenient time. All you need is to find a mirror and spend 5 minutes alone in front of it.

Early Results-

After the first few times you do it, you will feel a little difference in your behaviour but it may not last long. That's because when you leave the quiet room with the mirror, you go back to reality with its problems, meet the people who are mean and critical to you, you get disappointments and worries. Thus, you easily forget the way you felt while practicing confidence and continue the day as usual. But don't let that stop you. Start doing it twice a day, make it a habit and in a week or two you will see a more confident person in the reflection.

Ultimate Result-

The magic of mirror technique, however, happens in the long-term. After one or two months nobody will be able to deny that you are a different person. They will at least look and feel like one you expect about you. You would not be afraid to look people in the eyes anymore and will become more active, because you will spend more time to reaching the goals you've set. This time you will be absolutely sure that nothing will stop you simply because you won't let it get in your way.

The best result you will have from the exercise is the strength and power that your eyes are going to radiate. After that you will also notice how people treat you in a different way because you will not feel inferior to them anymore. Some may even feel afraid to argue with you as you seem so determined and confident.

Use this strategy and become an individual with strong character and self-esteem. Let the mirror be your friend. You will feel the difference by having great confidence in you.

81. Stick to your principles

Be conscious every day of the decisions you make, however big or small and how close they bring you to being the person you really want to become.

You should obey the principle without being bound by them.

Decide what you must change in your behaviour to align your life more closely to what you believe. Look at the choices you have made in your past and observe how much you have or have not lived by those principles. Maintaining hard earned good reputation and personal integrity is rewarding.

Choose a set of rules, morals, or principles that you believe. It will lead to a happy, satisfying and righteous life, and to a better world. You can obey the ethics of a particular religion, or you can develop you own, based on your experiences.

You will probably feel your self-confidence and personal strength growing as you face and overcome challenges while sticking to your values, whatever they may be. It is not what the world holds for you, it is what you bring to it.

82. Help others

Helping others is a good idea to feel satisfaction in life. This brings confidence with it. Although we all have busy lives, it is important to take some time and consider the well-being of others. If you can spare only a small portion of your time, you can perform volunteer work as a way to help others.

Helping others should be a natural extension of your responsibilities. Unfortunately, it doesn't come as easy as you would think.

Helping others is not always easy. It can sometimes derail your schedule and cost you time, money and other resources. It can even be interpreted the wrong way. However, keep these tips in mind for some easy ways to show your connections that they truly matter to you.

You can help others in many ways. Some of them are following-

1. Join the type of non-profit organization you wish to volunteer at. Most communities have food banks, shelters, hospitals, senior citizen centres and they are in need of volunteers. You can check your local phone book to find charitable organizations in your neighbourhood.

2. Help others in your neighbourhood. You can do more than volunteer for a charitable organization. *For example,* you can offer your help and company to an elderly couple who has no child to look after them. You can help an old neighbour to take her/him to doctor.

3. If you are joining an organization, let the organization know the time commitment, you can give them. You may not have the ability and time to volunteer on a frequent basis, but whatever time you can spare will be appreciated.

4. If you are wealthy enough to give money to the needy person, you can make a monetary donation. Not everyone has the time to volunteer at a non-profit organization. However, you can still help others by giving some money to charity. Start up a collection to make an even higher donation.

5. You can donate clothes, medicine, children toys and used clothes to charity organizations.

6. One of the easiest ways to help others is to simply share your knowledge. You do not have to be in front of a classroom to teach. Every day there is an opportunity to educate someone about your area of expertise. The key is to keep educating yourself so you can stay ahead.

7. The number one rule of helping people should be to find out what is actually valuable to someone. You may spend time and effort helping someone. Make an effort to ask them where they need help and keep that in mind when you see an opportunity.

8. Think about the resources you have invested in and try to share your resources to help others. Be mindful of whether they can help someone else. Keep your under or unused resources in the back of your mind and try to connect them to people who can use them.

You can help people by giving gifts. In case of flood, famine, or storm you can send food, clothes or others useful items. You should get them a gift that makes sense and will help them. People tend to remember who helped them when they were in need, so it is important to make an extra effort during these times.

83. Ignore Distractions

At work just as in life, distractions are par for the course. The key point is how well you manage them. Some of us get pushed off balance by the slightest interruptions at work, while others easily tune out distractions. The truth is, nobody is completely attentive to his work at all the time.

Distractions range from external annoyances like loud phone talkers in open cube space to self- distractions such as Face-book, personal E-mail, or surfing the Web.

There are a number of common workplace disruptions that many of us endure. Those include: unceasing e-mail, text messages, social media and other websites not related to work, personal calls, co-worker or client interruptions, last minute requests, unscheduled meetings, audible distractions *i.e.,* music, television, e-mail alerts, phones ringing, other people's phone conversations, noisy copy machines or printers, people or vehicles going by outside your window, elevator doors or restroom doors opening and closing, etc., gossiping co-workers, and micromanaging supervisors.

Moreover, your work-style habits can cause real distraction and are often masked as unavoidable work issues, like spending your day checking and answering email or prioritizing your day based on whatever comes across your desk, keeping you away from getting much of your other work done, it becomes dangerous.

All persons have trouble with distractions in the workplace to some degree. The key is to limit those distractions as much as possible. However, occasional workplace distractions can actually be a good thing. When distractions take up too much of your time and prevent you from getting your work done."

If interruptions in the office are not managed, they can seriously erode your ability to focus and may lead to factual mistakes and poor judgment, which can lead to poor performance. The result is you can lose confidence and can even lose your job.

Frequent distractions negatively affect your mood. They can prevent you from getting your work done on time, which creates more stress for you and consequently makes you more frustrated and unhappy at work.

Happiness largely comes from feeling that you are doing a good job at work that has meaning to you, and seeing positive results from your efforts. It takes skill and focus to produce high-quality work and you develop a sense of confidence.

Distractions can decrease focus, which increases stress, which can intensify any poor work habit you may have. Distractions can lead to poor performance, creating a negative spiral where poor performance leads to more stress which leads to more poor performance, and so on.

To avoid distractions, you should make sure you eat properly, sleep properly, drink plenty of water; take breaks from your screen, laugh and avoid short term stimuli like coffee and chocolate. By recognizing when you get distracted and what distracts you, you can learn to avoid these situations. Learn your patterns; when you work best and worst and make sure you make the most of your best time. You should ignore distraction. The first thing you need to understand is what you get distracted from. Then try to avoid these distractions.

84. Creative Life Helps Fulfill Your Life Purpose and Confidence

A creative life does not only include expressing traditional ideas of creativity such as painting, writing, or designing. Being creative also means approaching everything we do from a free-flowing, imaginative frame of mind. From raising children to saving money, everything we do can be done creatively. The more creative you can become in the everyday aspects of your life, the more your creative things start flowing.

http://www.choosing-life-my-way.com/discovery-session.html This will enable you to begin thinking of bigger and bolder means of creating new methods, new ideas, new models and even new masterpieces. There is no one way of developing creativity, but all ways come from an open and curious mind and heart.

Exploring your life purpose uncovers the areas in which you have special creative abilities.

One thing that following your purpose will definitely ensure is the development of a creative life. Life purpose and an urge to create, and to express our gifts and talents go hand in hand. We are born with a strong desire to be creative and to create.

To lead a creative and satisfying life, you should let yourself dream, explore, experiment, play, sing, dance, get out in nature, listen to beautiful music, burn scented candles, read, write, paint, sculpt and dream some more. You can try creative activities without worrying about technique, or trying to do it right. There is no right! Can you imagine if Picasso had worried about the traditional rules of art?

You need to rediscover your playful, innocent, joyful, creative nature. The childlike quality that we all possess, but most of us bury, is the essence of creativity. To live a creative life, open up your mind to the unlimited possibilities in any task or situation. Try doing things differently.

To really start living a creative life, think creatively about everything, not just 'creative' activities. Also, try as many creative activities as you can think of, and don't worry about being 'good at' them; just enjoy. Play more, do things differently and try doing some off-beat things you wouldn't normally do. Think, you are a creative person, you just need to let your creativity shine through and it will light up your life. This will fill you with a feeling of self-confidence and happiness.

85. Mind Your Language to Build Your Confidence

It is true that your outside voice really does affect your inner voice. Your language shapes how you experience any given moment. Mind your language by being aware of often you use disempowering phrases. It will help your mind to use language that builds your confidence.

Language isn't just thoughts and speech. Emotions are part of your language. How do you feel when you say "I don't know what to do"? Confused? Helpless? Incompetent? Lost? Alone? Angry? Frustrated? That's a lot of negative emotions.

The language you use in your thoughts and when you speak to others holds the power for building your confidence or undermining it. Did you know that that your inner voice is affected by the language you use when you are talking out loud? Did you know that you can influence your inner voice and get it to be more supportive of you?

Here are some examples of disempowering phrases that you may not be aware you are using. Even little things have a powerful impact on your confidence.

1. I'll never get this
2. I don't know what to do
3. This is too much for me
4. I'm stuck
5. This won't work

Your sub-conscious mind believes everything you say, it may be loud or in your head. So, when you say either to yourself or to someone else, "I don't know what to do", your sub-conscious mind believes it and operates based on that belief.

By changing your language to a positive statement such as "I'll have to figure this out" you give your sub-conscious mind something to focus on that it can solve. Your sub-conscious mind loves to solve problems. It will go to work helping you figure it out so you will know what to do. You will move forward to do it. It will work. You will be able to handle it. And you will get it done.

Pay attention to the emotions you are feeling when you are talking to yourself and to others. Practice changing your language to evoke positive emotions.

Here are examples of confidence-breaking phrases and their confidence building alternatives:

A player can say-

"I can't do what my coach wants me to do". Rather he should say "There's something I'm not getting yet. I can ask for more help and I can practice more. I know I will get it eventually."

"I can't afford swimming or dancing or riding lessons/ training", it should be "This is something that's really important to me. I need so much money for it. I just need to figure out a way to make that extra money."

Don't just re-phrase a negative into a positive by saying the exact opposite and then pretend everything is rosy. If you are afraid of something, it's ok to admit you are afraid. Empower yourself by saying something like "I am afraid, but I will get help".

To build your confidence, you must be honest and realistic. You should state the facts and the action you can take at the same time. Mind how you feel and create a positive emotion.

You should develop more awareness for how you talk to yourself and how you talk with others. Notice how often you use disempowering, negative phrases. Mind your language and your mind will support you in building your confidence.

86. Speak With Committed Language

Committed language is very special. It is an innate capacity that we all have. Committed language is when you speak directly, with your heart, with all parts of your mind supporting what you say. It means you speak from the 'Neutral Mind', having processed the thought with all three functional minds. Your self is committed to the impact of your words. Committed language is direct, truthful and spoken from your heart with full awareness of the other person, your roles, and obligations.

Some people think they are very clever. They think that they are so clever they can play games or they can lie or they feel that they are beautiful and wonderful people. They think that they can outsmart their own hollowness and suffer no reaction from all the lies they weave. The fact is that they shall be shallow and hollow forever. Do you think you think you can save yourself and harm somebody else? You have the choice to lie for the rest of your life. But each time you lie, you lose a piece of your self-confidence.

You feel you are an intelligent person who knows everything; you educate yourself, feed yourself, decorate yourself, wear clothes and accomplish great things. But when you cannot speak with a committed language of consciousness, it is very degrading to you. You feel shallow and look like an idiot when someone asks you, "Did you really say this? Is that what you meant?" You cannot accept or say yes or no. When you waver and cannot say directly what is true or real, then you fall before your own self. Without the neutral mind, you protect yourself with diversions, manipulations, and lies. This game of lies catches up with you. When that happens, it brings an end to your personality. It brings an end to your psyche and your projection. It brings an end to the flow of your confidence. **Whenever you lie it takes away a chunk from you that is called self-confidence.** Instead of lies, practice the art of committed language so you can tap the power and beauty of your mind.

Normally you do not speak with committed language. The result is your love is not committed, your compassion is not committed, and your relationships are not committed. Uncommitted relationships are very painful. There is fear, no trust, unconscious anger, and mistake after mistake. You try to bury the shallowness you feel. You have no depth because you are not committed. Without commitment in your language and actions you feel that you do not know what is going on. You are unsure and lack control. You react by feeling irritation and anger. Then you find lots of ways to let that anger out. One of the worst and most common ways is to harm you by lying.

A lie is nothing but a habit. It takes away confidence and it comes from a lack of confidence. It is a vicious circle of insecurity and pain. If you don't want to say something, don't say. You do not have to lie. Instead just speak up, "I don't want to say it." It takes courage to say, "I don't want to say it." But that courage builds your confidence.

87. Learn Managing Stress

You experience stress if you believe that you don't have the time, resources, or knowledge to handle a situation. In short, you experience stress when you feel "out of control."

This means that different people handle stress differently, in different situations. You can handle stress better if you're confident in your abilities, if you can change the situation to take control, and if you feel that you have the help and support needed to do a good job.

Many of us experience stress in life, whether this is in the short term from one of the projects, or long-term stress from a high-pressure career. This can be profoundly unpleasant. It can seriously affect your health and your work. However, it is possible to manage stress, if you use the right tools and techniques.

You have two instinctive reactions that make up your stress response. These are the "fight or flight" response, and the General Adaptation Syndrome (GAS). Both of these reactions can happen at the same time.

Our brains release stress hormones that prepare the body to either "fly" from the threat or "fight" it. This energizes us, but it also makes us excited, anxious, and irritable. In these types of situations, a calm, rational, controlled and socially-sensitive approach is often more appropriate than to try other hurried up methods.

When you encounter a situation, you make two judgments. *First,* you decide whether the situation is threatening – this could be a threat to your social standing, values, time, or reputation, as well as to our survival. This can then trigger the fight or flight response. Next thing you do, you judge whether you have the resources to meet the perceived threat. These resources can include time, knowledge, emotional capabilities, energy, strength and much more. How stressed you feel then, it depends on how it is out of control, you feel and how well you can meet the threat with the resources you have available.

Consequences of Stress

Stress impacts your ability to do your jobs effectively. It also affects how you work with other people. This can have a serious impact on your careers and well as on our general well-being and relationships.

Long-term stress can also cause poor health conditions. It may cause many serious diseases also.

Signs of Stress

Everyone reacts to stress differently. However, some common signs and symptoms of the stress are:

1. Obsessive or compulsive behaviour.

2. Constant fatigue.

3. Persistent difficulty in concentrating.

4. Consistent feelings of being overwhelmed or overloaded.

5. Irritability and angry attitude.

6. Significant weight gain or loss.

7. Frequent headaches.

8. Excessive sleeping or insomnia.

9. Cold or sweaty hands and feet.

10. Frequent heartburn, stomach pain, or nausea.

11. Panic attacks.

12. Social withdrawal or isolation.

How to Manage Stress

The first step in managing stress is to understand where these feeling are coming from. You should identify the causes of frequent stress in your life. Next stress is, list these stressors in order of their impact. Try to know which affect your health and well-being most and which affect your work and productivity?

Follow these things to minimize stress-

1. You should learn managing Your Time. Your workload can cause stress if you don't manage your time well. This can be a key source of stress for very many people.

2. You should avoid multitasking. You should only check email only at certain times and don't use electronic devices for a while before going to bed, so that you use this time to "switch off" fully.

3. Workspace stress can come from irritating, frustrating, uncomfortable or unpleasant conditions in the workplace. Take action to minimize stress in your working environment.

4. Emotion-oriented approaches are useful when the stress you're experiencing comes from the way that you perceive a situation. It can be annoying for people to say this, but a lot of stress comes from overly- negative thinking

5. You should use cognitive restructuring, thought awareness, rational thinking and positive thinking to change the way that you perceive stressful events.

6. Some people experience stress because they are maladaptive perfectionists, who struggle to complete tasks

unless they complete them perfectly. Others experience stress because they have a fear of failure.

7. You can use techniques like meditation and physical relaxation to calm yourself when you feel stressed.

8. You should get enough exercise and sleep and learn how to make the most of your down time, so that you can recover from stressful events.

9. You should take advantage of your support network. This could include your friends and family, as well as people at work and professional providers, such as counsellors or family doctors.

Remember things about stress:-

We experience stress when we feel threatened, and when we believe that we don't have the resources to deal with a challenging situation. After some time, this can cause long-term health problems; and it can also affect the quality of our work and our productivity.

To control your stress, you should conduct a job analysis, so that you know your most priorities at work. Learn good time management strategies, so that you can handle your priorities effectively. Try to let go of negative thinking habits and become a positive thinker by using affirmations and visualization.

88. Improve Your Self-Confidence through Body language

With all the pressures, demands and competitiveness of modern life any boost is very important in life. Did you know that something as simple as body language could actually improve your self-confidence? Most of us know that body language can influence how other perceives us, but it can also affect how we see ourselves. To develop confidence, you should look no further than own your body. We all know that body language is a form of communication.

We know that our body language can send a message to others. Do you notice a difference in the way you feel when you stand tall with an open posture versus being in a closed off or fatal position? You should try it and see for yourself. You'll likely notice a difference. How you carry yourself can affect your mood along with your self-confidence.

Your body language can actually shape who you are. Practicing power poses for as little as two minutes can make you feel more confident, more relaxed and even reduce stress hormones. At the same time it boosts testosterone (considered the power hormone) in both men and women. So in effect, by practicing confident power poses you change your brain chemistry. Once you change your brain chemistry, you change your thoughts and perceptions about yourself. That is empowering and leads to greater self-confidence.

You should be conscious of any small postures you may inadvertently be displaying. Look about the way you stand or sit? Are your shoulders rounded or is your head down? What about arms and legs- are they crossed? All these poses are indicative of weakness and vulnerability, so try to avoid them when building self-confident body language.

Adopting dominant poses can not only change the way others see you, but it can change the way you see yourself. You will see yourself as capable and confident.

89. Make Planning and Preparation for the unknown

People often feel less confident about new or potentially difficult situations. Perhaps the most important factor in developing confidence is planning and preparing for the unknown.

For example, if you are applying for a new job, you would be wise to prepare for the interview. Plan what you would want to say in the interview and think about some of the questions that you may be asked. Practise your answers with friends or colleagues and gain their feedback. This will give you confidence in the interview.

There can be many other examples of planning for an interview. How are you going to travel to the interview? How long will the journey take? What should you wear? Take control of unknown situations the best you can, breakdown tasks into smaller sub-tasks and plan as many as you can.

In the same way you should make a planning for your future schemes and life's achievement. You should get goal to find out new horizons. When you do preparation in advance, this will create more chances of success and you will gain confidence.

90. Sleep Impacts Your Self-Esteem and Self-Confidence

Running on too little sleep can have detrimental effects on your mind, body and brain. For years you have known that sleep deprivation is bad for our mental and physical health. Now alarming research has linked lack of sleep to higher stress, low self-esteem, physical health issues and even brain damage.

You should always remember that sleep deprivation wears down your normal capacity to deal with daily aggravations and challenges, causing the cycle of stress to wear you down. One night of disrupted sleep lowers the threshold for "stress perception." When you are dead tired, or have had weeks of restless nights, frustration and feeling frazzled makes you less capable and less effective in your day to day life. Sleep loss can lead to irreversible damage.

For many people, it's nearly impossible to get enough sleep. Not just because they can't find the time, but their brains don't shut off once they hit the bed. Over-thinking about the day, being alone with your thoughts, and dreading another sleepless night add to the mix of stress. Hectic schedules make it hard to get the things one needs.

Sleep deprivation increases your odds of feeling overly sensitive. *For example,* if your friend does not text back for hours, it may start to get under your skin, leading to feelings of fear or frustration, and more self-doubt. Add in more sleepless nights and you are set up to feel less connected to yourself and your goals and more sensitive to the outside world.

Relationship problems with friends or family can be created by lack of sleep. Letting little things get to you amplifies emotions that you normally would push away, making you less happy with yourself and a partner, which can create a major hit to your confidence.

Irritability becomes more prevalent in your life. You have less patience for people, situations, and often act out or get angry at yourself for feelings frustration. **Increased depression or sadness can develop with lack of sleep** which often contributes to low self-confidence. Those who are already depressed or have other underlying mental health disorders may find those problems exacerbated by lack of sleep.

Ways to get good Sleep and Improve Self-Esteem

1. Do any amount of mindful meditation every day. This can simply be sitting and observing your thoughts with a compassionate, non-judgmental attitude.

2. Incorporate more breaks and gentle exercise to get your brain "reset." When you do this, the noise in your mind is not as amplified at night. It may seem "impossible" to break away from the daily grind but 5-10 minutes here and there have been shown to recharge your brain.

3. Avoid TV, phone, tablet, e-mails, your Instagram feed, and video games in bed. The light and any activity stimulate neurotransmitter activity. Falling asleep with the TV on will disrupt your sleep cycle.

4. Wind up for one hour before bedtime. Ideally this would be restorative time like, relaxed reading, bath, or mediation practice. This is something to induce the relaxation response hypnosis on soothing music. Don't use electronics an hour before bed.

5. If you have trouble falling asleep due to your thoughts,

write them down, thank your mind for reminding you about it and tell your brain that you will address it tomorrow.

6. Make your room hibernation friendly. A cool, cozy, and dark room makes your body go into hibernation mode. Make sure your bedroom is quiet and your comforters are comfy to help you feel relaxed when you go into bed.

7. Decrease caffeine as it exacerbates anxiety and can create disturbances in your sleep patterns. Coffee, tea, soda, energy drinks and chocolate, remain in the body on average from three to five hours but they can affect some people up to 12 hours later. Even if you do not think caffeine affects you, it may be disrupting and changing the quality of your sleep.

The more consistent your sleep cycle is the better you will feel. Do try and keep your bedtime and wake time consistent. You should always remember that disrupted sleep can hurt your self-esteem and self-confidence and can make you more stressed.

91. Get Healthy and Stay Healthy for Greater Confidence

Here, are essential elements of good health. If you take care of the things you will be much healthier and this will be the reason for developing self-confidence in you.

1. **You should do something physically active-**

Regular moderate daily physical activity goes a long way to help us maintain and improve our fitness, as well as our sense of well-being. Here, are a few ideas to help you find ways to stay active every day-

1. Find an activity you really enjoy and you are more likely to do it more often. Go out dancing. Join a sports team like ultimate Frisbee or softball. Go rollerblading or bicycling. Play more often.

2. Walking is one of the best forms of exercise and almost anyone can do it. A recent study found that people who walked their dog 20 minutes daily 5 days a week lost 8 kg in one year and improved their flexibility and balance. They also felt more positive and energetic.

3. You can be more active with your household chores. Do vigorous housework. You can listen to music and dance in your living room.

4. You should participate in yoga and fitness classes to improve your fitness: Many local gyms, in addition to weights and treadmills, offer classes such as step aerobics and stretching. If scheduling your activity works better for you, consider which activity speaks to you and go for it.

2. You should eat a healthy breakfast

1. A healthy breakfast is the cornerstone of a good diet. It is a meal that provides the opportunity to eat a serving of whole grains, a digestible protein. The energy from a healthy breakfast can carry you through your morning in a more stable way than by eating stimulating foods such as sweets and coffee.

2. If you are trying to improve your diet and nutrition and stay healthy as you age, eat a good breakfast every day. Vary your foods and try to get some protein if you have problems regulating your blood sugar.

3. People can lower their cholesterol by eating breakfast. This is due to several factors. Breakfasts tend to be high in fibber like fruit, oatmeal, whole grain cereals which absorb cholesterol in the intestines for removal from the body.

More importantly, however, when we skip breakfast, our bodies go for 10-16 hours with no outside source of energy. Our chemistry begins to shift to a mode of starvation, which increases appetite and changes how our bodies regulate blood sugar. We then tend to crave high fat and high carbohydrate foods and binge later in the day, resulting in taking in more calories than we need just as our bodies are primed to store energy in the form of fat.

3. You should eat Fruits and Vegetables

Fruits and vegetables supply many nutrients that are important for your health. *For example,* the orange colour of carrots and sweet potatoes indicate their high levels of beta-carotene which the body converts into vitamin A. This vitamin is important for healthy skin and eyes. Spinach is a good source of vitamin A, vitamin C, iron and calcium. All fruits and vegetables supply the body with fibber needed for cholesterol regulation and proper bowel function.

1. You should include dark green leafy vegetables every day.

2. You should emphasize vegetables in your meals, and choose fruits for snacks or dessert.

3. The brightest and deepest colours indicate the highest levels of nutrients.

4. You should eat a variety of plant parts: leaves, stems, roots, flowers and fruit.

5. At lunch and dinner, you should aim for half of your plate being vegetables.

4. You can take a Good Quality Multivitamin Supplement

1. Eating a health-promoting diet is an essential component of good health. While it seems to be common sense that eating a healthy diet provides all of the vitamins and minerals we need to enjoy good health and reduce the risk of chronic disease. Numerous scientific studies have shown that using good quality nutritional supplements can go beyond addressing nutrient deficiencies and help you

achieve optimal health.

2. It is found that daily use of a multivitamin by older adults is a relatively inexpensive yet potentially powerful way to stay healthy..

A good quality supplement contains higher levels of antioxidant vitamins and minerals. It also balances the minerals and vitamins in proper ratios for absorption and utilization by the body. Vitamins and minerals should be in safe amounts and chemical forms that absorb well and are easily utilized by the body.

5. You should drink plenty of Water

1. Generally we get water in many foods we eat and beverages we drink. Pure water is often the best form to ingest. Adequate water is an extremely inexpensive and efficacious health practice.

2. Water is the drink of the wise man. Water is fundamental to all life on earth. Our bodies are made up of 60% water. It is involved in every function in the body, including circulation, digestion, absorption of nutrients and the transmission of electrical currents in the body which control our nerves, muscles and hormones. Due to its importance in proper elimination and detoxification, it is said "The solution to pollution is dilution, "as water facilitates the elimination of waste products through urination, sweating, defecation, tears and mucus which line our respiratory and digestive tracts.

3. Water quality is very important. In many areas of the country, tap water may contain lead, radon, nitrates and other potentially toxic chemicals. Additionally chlorine and chloramines are placed in municipal water to decontaminate it.

92. Express Your Emotions Appropriately

Emotional factors play an important role in health and illness. Seven emotions that particularly affect the body: joy, anger, sadness, grief, pensiveness, fear and fright. These emotions are not by themselves thought to be pathological and all constitute emotional aspects of healthy people. However, if any of these emotions are excessive over a long period of time or arises suddenly with great force, it can generate imbalances and illness.

Inappropriate expression of emotions leads to physical and mental symptoms. *For example,* inappropriate expression of anger is thought to affect the Liver. People who feel frustrated or irritable are often not expressing their underlying anger appropriately by talking about it or by creating change in their lives to relieve their frustration. Consequently, this can lead to depression, aches in the body, constipation and inappropriate outbursts of anger.

Holding in emotions or expressing them in inappropriate ways can lead to health imbalances which may lead to illness. In our society, this takes awareness and careful choices of words as the expression of "negative" emotions such as anger or sadness is often discouraged socially. Nonetheless, it is important to be in touch with our feelings and to express them in an authentic way.

Learning to be in touch with emotions, expressing ourselves appropriately and letting things go-it is not easy but produces rewards in enriching our emotional lives and our relationships and connections with others and than making your life healthy. This will naturally improve your self-confidence.

93. Have some Recreation

All work and no play make you a dull person. This saying has lasted from long time and for good reasons. If you work all the time and don't have time for some occasional recreation, you will simply tire yourself. Recreation is beneficial for both physical and psychological well-being.

Recreation is about engaging in delightful activities that bring in happiness. It is very important to understand the necessity of recreation and giving some time for it.

Recreation is the spending of time in pleasurable activities. Engaging ourselves in activities that invite happiness and peace of mind is nothing but recreation. Recreation can be in the form of rest, entertainment or adventure. Recreation means to take a refreshing break from the monotony of life. With the increasing pace of life, we have become the participants of a never-ending race. In the fast life of today, you have become too busy to take out time for your near and dear ones. You have become so engrossed with work that you hardly get time to peep into your own self. You have no time to introspect; you have no time to interact.

Recreation is an activity, rather an opportunity to take a break, the much-needed break from work. If you are thinking of going on an outing this weekend or planning for a trip with close friends, you should go ahead, for you need recreation.

Importance of Recreation

Recreation is moreover the time to get together to have fun. Devoting some time for recreation on a daily basis helps in the long run in maintaining health and achieving a peace of mind. You can participate in some regular physical activity, play a sport or exercise. These recreational activities serve as a means of relaxation. Research has shown that recreation on a daily basis reduces risks of diabetes and hypertension, enhances physical and mental health and improves the quality of life.

The excitement and thrill that accompanies adventure sports adds to the freshness. Sports make you feel challenged, encourage you to take risks, exhibit your skills, thus building self-confidence. **The activities of recreation result in the enhancement of your interpersonal and intrapersonal skills.** Apart from being a way of spending free time, recreation is a way to socialize. It is a way of being with the loved ones and enjoy. Recreation gives you an opportunity to meet new people and develop new friendships.

Recreational activities are widely popular across the globe. Some people enjoy touring to beautiful places around the world, while others take interest in pursuing their hobbies as a means of recreation. Be it of any sort, recreation needs to be made a vital component of the fast life.

Values and Benefits of Recreation-

1. It Reduces Stress.
2. It Helps You Relax.
3. **It has Social Benefits:** It helps you meet like minded people and develop a favourable rapport.
4. **It creates quality of Life:** Recreational activities help you build **self-esteem and confidence.** It helps you enhance

the quality of life by **building a positive self-image.**

5. **It Sharpens Skills:** You not only are inclined to learn more things but are also motivated to be at your best.

6. **It creates new Avenues:** It has happened to people and it can help you too. People who enjoy it to the best of its form have developed a career in one form or the other.

7. **It makes effective Time Utilization:** When your body is at the better of its form both in terms of health and energy, recreational activities helps you utilize your time effectively.

8. Recreation activities are best mechanism to refill your energy and make you feel alive again.

9. It refreshes the senses.

10. Recreational activities have a very good impact on your health.

Conclusion-

Recreation feels like a rain shower during scorching heat. Recreation is the time to be together with your friends and family and to have fun. Devoting some time for recreation helps in staying healthy and achieving a peace of mind. Recreational activities serve as a way of relaxing and as researches have shown recreation on a daily basis reduces risks of diabetes and hypertension and it improves mental and physical health and improves the quality of life and then develops your self-confidence.

94. Interact with people for Social Confidence

In every social group and every social interaction, there is always a leader. Being social and interacting with people can be fun, engaging and exciting; however for many it can also be scary, exhausting and raise levels of anxiousness. However, to be clear there is no magic pill that makes you feels more confident in social situations.

Social leadership is another key point. Being the leader in a social situation enables you to fully be yourself, show your uniqueness and your excellence and it enables you to truly live the life that you want, as you can direct the flow of conversation and events.

Enhancing your social confidence not only helps you live the life that you truly want, but it helps deepen your relationships with others. It can help enhance your career or work life and ultimately it will help you become a happier person. Social interactions and relationships are keys to happiness, so it is worth the time and effort gaining an understanding of how to develop yourself to ensure you gets the best out of your relationships.

95. Join a Meet up group

Meet up groups are fantastic way of meeting new people. They are a encouraging you of practicing social interaction in a comfortable environment. There are always new people coming to Meet up groups and that you will find that you will never be the only person that does not know anyone. This can help you to start to create your very own social circle that you can practice taking the lead in.

Starting your own Meet up group is also a fantastic way of enabling you to truly show your uniqueness. You can create your group's site and pick the locations. You can choose your target audience, allowing you to build social leadership in a way that is suited to your life.

You can develop and deliver a presentation on your topic of expertise and enhance your social confidence and social leadership. Giving a presentation enables you to practice your speaking and communication skills in front of an audience. It also helps you develop authority in the topic that you are choosing.

You will notice that after giving a presentation, people seem more interested in talking to you. Getting up and presenting in front of an audience gives others an insight into who you are as a person, enabling them to feel more comfortable in approaching you. This enables you to easily develop your social confidence amongst others that you have expertise in and in an environment where you feel more comfortable.

96. Go to various events

You can go to networking events or singles events to develop confidence. Having complete social confidence and social leadership is not something that is found overnight. It is built and developed from taking action, putting yourself out there, learning more about yourself and experiencing the world. What are you going to do today that helps enhance your social confidence and social leadership?

There is a lot of stigma around networking events, but in saying that there is also a lot of awesome value. Networking events are everywherqe these days and for a range of different purposes. You can find a networking event that suits your interests and practice meeting new people. The more that you practice interacting with others and the more you observe others interacting. Then you will quickly build your social confidence and also enhance your social leadership. This will allow you to be more comfortable in expressing who you truly are.

Even if you're not single, you can go to single's events. It can be a fantastic way of putting yourself out there and practicing your social skills. The good thing is, everyone is there to meet new people and simply have a good time.

The other way is you can be the organizer of events among your friends. You already have a good relationship with your friends and you will no doubt have social confidence amongst them. Being the organizer of events is a great way of developing your social leadership, allowing you to show your uniqueness and do activities that most interest you and that you feel more comfortable in doing. Your friends will be helping you to develop your social confidence.

97. Overcoming Shyness to Feel More Confident

"Each time we face a fear, we gain strength, courage and confidence in the doing."

Once you get a better understanding of social dynamics it becomes a lot easier to make friends and increase your social circles, no matter where in the world you are.

Sometimes people can be quick to judge and label based on stereotypes and perceptions. Not everyone will take the time to reach out to you and get to know you before they label you.

A Few Tips:

1. One of the best ways to overcome shyness is to make it a habit of speaking to everyone.

Since you need to have confidence to be able to speak to people and you need to speak to people to build confidence. The trick is to start small, *for example,* just start saying "hello" or "good morning" to one person every day.

Then when you start feeling more comfortable with this, start speaking to two people every day and increase the length of your conversations.

Don't limit yourself to speaking to people you know or "click" with. Talk to everyone in your community, talk to men, women, young, old, whether they seem normal, strange, or crazy - even if it's just to say hello. Many people won't take the initiative to get to know you, so that just means you have to get to know them and give them the chance to get to know you.

You'll find that the majority of people who you start a conversation with are really friendly. If you remember this, reaching out to someone new won't seem so scary.

98. Don't Pay heed to all spoken words

You should also take no heed unto all words that are spoken. Here, your wisdom can lead to right conduct. You should not pay serious attention to evil reports either about yourself or others, nor regulate your views and actions according to such distortions of the truth. To be always hankering to know what people say of you is to set-up a false standard, which will assuredly lead you astray as you probably shall find, that they do not take you at your own valuation, but they thoroughly mark your weaknesses.

No man is wise at all times. Sometimes foolish words and unguarded expressions may drop from him, which it is better to take no notice of. These expressive words should not be strictly attended to, and closely examined, since they will not bear importance. A person should not listen to everything that is said of him or others. You should not curiously inquire what others say of you; and what you yourself hear. You should take no notice of; it is often best to let it pass, and not call it over again. By rehearsing a matter, or taking up words spoken, a lot of trouble and mischief may follow. A person should not "give his heart" to it. You should not give your mind to what is said of you, but should be careless and indifferent about it, otherwise you may meditate for revenge.

99. Learn to Control Your Will Power

A person with a strong will power can face adversity will courage, believe in his abilities and would not be dissuaded from achieving his dreams. People with strong will power are ready to face all kinds of obstacles and hindrances. An important factor that has contributed substantially to the success of all great people is their will power.

If it were not for will power, would Mahatma Gandhi have taken on to oppose an empire that ruled far and wide around the world? Yes it was will power of Mother Teresa who brought solace to thousands of destitute dying people on the streets?

Control on will power is very important in life. It can make ordinary people extraordinary people. They have do extraordinary will power. God has endowed everyone with the will to succeed. It depends upon the individual how you would like to develop it; one can develop one's will power with determination. As a player or cricketer learns the tricks of game with his will power, he succeeds in life.

You should get out of your comfort zone and ensure that you do a little more than is expected of you. The will power slowly develops to give you enhanced self-confidence. Learn to tell yourself that nothing is impossible, I will complete this work. I will do it successfully.

100. Learn to listen patiently

It is a fact that People prefer speaking to listening. Generally people are poor listeners. One of the biggest hurdles in communicating effectively is that people are poor listeners.

Look, what happens generally. When a person is trying to communicate a message to another person, even before the first person has completed what he or she has to say, the second person is ready with a reply without fully understanding what the message was trying to convey. Think about this situation. This communication can never be effective.

With the mind involved in preparing to respond, it fails to listen to the complete message. With a premature response ready, the listener interrupts causing the communication to become ineffective. This way, neither the message can be received completely nor will the response be correct or up to the point.

The solution to this problem lies in learning to be patient listener. You should hear everything that is communicated correctly. When you hear carefully, you will be able to relate it appropriately to your knowledge and past experiences related to the matter. This way your response will always be appropriate. You should learn to become a good listener if you would like to be responsible. This will enhance your self-confidence, because you will know the effect matter and its solution.

101. A Confident Person Should Remember

You should follow the following things to most interactions with your friends, colleagues, family, customers and everybody else. You should always use common sense and try to behave as appropriately as possible, taking into account if any cultural differences.

1. **Say hello to people –**

You should greet people appropriately; gain eye contact and smile naturally, shake hands or hug where appropriate. You should but say hello to people, especially to colleagues and other people you see every day.

2. **Try to remember things about the other person and comment appropriately -**

You should remember and use their spouse's name, their birthday, and any significant events that have occurred in their life. Always be mindful of others' problems and difficult life events.

3. **Always use 'please' and 'thank you'-**

You should make sure to thank people for their input or contribution and always include 'please' when asking for something. If somebody offers you something so 'Yes please' or 'No thank you'.

4. **Always take time to make some small talk –**

You can mention the weather or ask about the other person's family or talk about something that is in the news.

Make an effort to engage in light conversation, show some interest, but don't overdo it. Remain friendly and positive and pick up on the verbal and non-verbal signals from the other person.

5. **Use appropriate language –**

You should be respectful to gender, race, religion, political viewpoints and other potentially controversial or difficult subjects. Do not make derogatory or potentially inflammatory comments or remarks.

6. **Praise and congratulate others on their achievements-**

You should remember that praise needs to be seen as genuine. this can be difficult if you feel jealous or angry.

7. **Learn to listen attentively –**

You should pay attention to others while they speak, do not get distracted mid-conversation and do not interrupt.

8. **Be polite and helpful to your subordinates as well as your bosses-**

You should respect and acknowledge the positions, roles and duties of others.

9. **Respect other people's time-**

You should try to be precise and to-the-point in explanations without appearing to be rushed.

10. **Apologise for your mistakes-**

If you say or do something that may be considered rude or embarrassing then you should apologise, but don't over do your apologies.

11. **Be assertive when necessary-**

But you should respect the right of others to be assertive.

12. Avoid gossip-

Try to have positive things to say about other people.

13. Dress appropriately for the situation-

You should avoid wearing revealing clothing in public and avoid staring at others who are wearing revealing clothing. You should try being dressed casually for the situation.

14. Avoid vocabulary that may be difficult for others to understand –

You should explain complex ideas or instructions carefully. Do not appear arrogant.

15. Respect and listen others-

You should be prepared to listen to, the ideas and opinions of others.

16. Always practise good table manners-

When eating around others. You should avoid foods with strong odours, do not talk with your mouth full or chew with your mouth open and eat quietly.

17. Avoid bad manner and behaviour-

Do not pick your nose or ears, chew on your fingers or bite your fingernails in public. Also avoid playing excessively with your hair.

18. Use humour carefully-

You should aim not to cause any offence and know the boundaries of appropriate language for different situations.

19. Practise good personal hygiene-

You should wash and brush your teeth regularly, change your clothes and use deodorant. Avoid strong perfumes, after-shaves or colognes.

20. Be punctual-

If you have arranged to meet somebody at a certain time make sure you are on time, or even a few minutes early. If you are going to be late let the other person/people know as far in advance as you can. Do not rely on feeble or exaggerated excuses to explain lateness. Respect other people's time and don't waste it.

21. Behave well and have good Manners-

Good manners cost nothing but can make a big difference to how other people feel about you, or the organisation you are representing. When you're polite and show good manners others are more likely to be polite and courteous in return.

You can improve your face-to-face or interpersonal relationships with others in many different ways.

❑❑❑

31. Self-Help to English Conversation
32. The Art of Effective Communication
33. A Book of Proverbs & Quotations
34. Word Power Made Easy
35. English Grammar Easier Way
36. General English for Competitive Examinations
37. Spoken English
38. School Essays, Letters Writing and Phrases
39. How to Write & Speak Better English
40. Quote Unquote (A Handbook of Famous Quotations)
41. Improve Your Vocabulary
42. Common Errors in English
43. The Art of Effective Letter Writing
44. Synonyms & Antonyms
45. Idioms
46. Business Letters

Lotus PRESS
Unit No. 220, 2nd Floor, 4735/22, Prakash Deep Building,
Ansari Road, Darya Ganj, New Delhi- 110002
Ph.: 23280047, 9811594448
E-mail : lotuspress1984@gmail.com, www.lotuspress.co.in

Other Books on

QUIZ & CAREERS

1. Lotus General Knowledge
2. 100 Ways to Develop Self Confidence **(New)**
3. 100 Ways to Motivate Yourself **(New)**
4. How to Solve Math Puzzles
5. History Quiz Book
6. Lotus Mathematics Quiz Book
7. The Great Book of Riddles & Jokes
8. How to Improve Your IQ
9. Learn to Play Chess Tactics & Strategies
10. World's Greatest Puzzles
11. Brain Ticklers in Economics
12. Brain Ticklers in Mathematics
13. Brain Ticklers in Nature
14. Brain Ticklers in General Knowledge
15. Brain Ticklers in English
16. Quiz for All
17. 1010 Riddles
18. Science Quiz
19. World Quiz
20. Facing Job Interviews
21. Preparing for Call Center Interviews
22. Sure Success in Interviews
23. Jokes for All

Lotus PRESS

Unit No. 220, 2nd Floor, 4735/22, Prakash Deep Building,
Ansari Road, Darya Ganj, New Delhi- 110002
Ph.: 23280047, 9811594448
• E-mail : lotuspress1984@gmail.com, www.lotuspress.co.in